Sheepdogs Among the Flock
The Art of Assisting Your Pastor

William C. Canfield

If anyone has the experience and knowledge to write a book concerning serving and faithfulness, it is Elder Bill Canfield. I have known him personally all the years he has served at World Harvest Church, and he has proven himself to be an Elisha. Every pastor longs for and needs a helper such as this. His years of experience give insight into the much-needed ministry of helps. This book offers understanding, direction, and revelation.

Pastor Darlene Bishop Driscoll
Solid Rock Church
Monroe, Ohio

Sheepdogs Among the Flock: The Art of Assisting Your Pastor is a must-have for every pastor and ministry leader. Elder William C. Canfield is no novice to serving his pastor. He is the real deal! This book is a pastor's friend and a guide for those who desire to serve well...exactly what the church needs today. It is the manuscript for those truly called to lead — on being contented in serving, staying connected to your leader, and remaining loyal in the fulfilling of your assignment.

Dealing with the ailments and trepidation that may arise while assisting your pastor, this volume is your answer key. I wholeheartedly endorse this book and admonish you to share it with every pastor and ministry leader you know. Let this script craft you into becoming the best *Sheepdog* you can be! Thank God for this book!

Dr. Medina Pullings
United Nations Church International
Richmond, Virginia

Elder Bill Canfield of World Harvest Church in Columbus, Ohio is one of the most profound, but genuine and stable gifts to the body of Christ. His expertise on the subject of this book is without contest. Not many in Christendom can say they have served a notable worldwide ministry for the span of three decades. Even fewer are able to serve with the same level of enthusiasm as they did when they began. Bill Canfield has accomplished both, working and supporting the ministry he serves with the highest level of dedication. The information in this book is a must for every individual who works in any area of ministry, whether paid staff or volunteer.

One of the greatest detriments to churches is misunderstanding or even mistreatment between pastors, leaders and congregational members. It often results in irreparable offenses and disillusionment. It's one of the enemy's greatest tactics to hinder the work of the Lord. We highly encourage every believer to read and receive the rich wisdom in this book that will enable them to become a greater asset to the Kingdom of God. Not only do we know that Elder Bill Canfield is among the most anointed and qualified vessels to write such a book, but we also have come to know his impeccable character and manner of life. Our family also considers him a dear friend who has helped us both personally and in our ministry.

Pastors Hank and Brenda Kunneman
Lord of Hosts Church and
One Voice Ministries
Omaha, Nebraska

When it comes to assisting a pastor, no one does it better than Elder Bill Canfield! One only has to observe Elder Canfield to learn what it means to serve. This book will be a much-needed answer to the prayers of pastors who have been longing for relief. Contained within its pages is a treasure trove of wisdom and insight from a man whose heart beats for God and His anointed servant, the pastor.

Pastor Eric Petree
City Gate Church
Lebanon, Ohio

Sheepdogs Among the Flock is an essential handbook for today's body of Christ, drafted by an experienced *Sheepdog*. In a way that is clear and easy to understand, Elder Canfield shares from his decades of expertise serving alongside a pastor who has touched hundreds of thousands of lives. For centuries, we have focused on the *shepherd* and the *sheep*. Now, there is a guide designed to instruct and inspire the *Sheepdog*, the pastor's helper.

Pastor Marion Dalton, Jr.
Bethel Harvest Church
Nicholasville, Kentucky

In this book, Elder Canfield has written what he has lived all these years. The subject is long overdue. The right man has written the right book at the right time and the right people—the body of Christ—must read it.

Eastwood Anaba
Eastwood Anaba Ministries
Ghana

It is a rare occasion for someone in the body of Christ to be able to view the full spectrum of ministry from leadership to all team members. In the many years I have known Bill Canfield, he is just that man. Bill knows the navigational route and the cooperation it takes to make the journey. This book is certain to guide you down the road less traveled.

Pastor Tommy Bates
Community Family Church
Independence, Kentucky

Elder Canfield is one of the most qualified leaders to discuss loyalty and longevity. He has been and continues to be a shining example of both, as he has served Pastor Rod Parsley now for over 35 years. I personally am overwhelmed with gratitude that he would take the lessons learned from these years of service and share them with such clarity and power. This is a must-read for every pastor, leader and lay minister, as well as for every member of every church. The principles expounded upon in this book will help establish a culture in your church and ministry that will bring sustained success.

Pastor Jonathan Miller
New Beginnings Church
Orlando, Florida

It was the fall of 1997 when I met a man who would literally alter the course of my life forever. Serving as an elder for one of America's leading ministries and also as a cornerstone of their Bible College, Elder Bill Canfield has taught through inspiration, information, and example and has been used by God to form thousands of young ministers into spiritual giants. I could think of no one more suited to write a book on serving their pastor than Elder Canfield.

In all my travels and in over 20 years of ministry, I have met no one who has served as faithfully in one ministry as has Elder Canfield. In his new book, *Sheepdogs Among the Flock,* Elder Canfield explores the importance of genuine servanthood in the body of Christ. Learning how to serve God's appointed leader with excellence and integrity is essential for any healthy church. The pastor MUST have men like Elder Canfield and in this new book, he points his fellow sheepdogs in the paths in which they must travel.

Pastor Shawn Coley
Destination Church
Kearneysville, West Virginia

A vitally needed book written by a man of God who has walked and modeled the principles He expounds. This writing will contribute to pastors achieving more, gaining greater vision and at the same time, having a quality of life. Not an oxymoron! All of God's sheepdogs must learn from this text and share in the mandate to perpetuate the succession plan of Christ.

Dr. Dean Radtke
Ministry Institute
Salisbury, North Carolina

In a time in Christendom where seemingly we have more "social clubs" than real, verified and bona fide churches—*which is largely due to the power struggles amongst the leaders in them*—it is refreshing to read a book that is timely and relevant on the subject of secondary leadership.

I encourage everyone who feels the call to lead within the confines of the local church to read and study this informative, educational and instructional masterpiece. In just the first few chapters, you will become empowered as a *Sheepdog*, and by the final chapter, you will recognize and embody the spirit of a *True Assistant* to your pastor.

Prophet Antonio Burroughs
Antonio Burroughs Ministries
Miami, Florida

Elder Bill Canfield epitomizes what it means to be a *sheepdog*, someone who serves the vision by putting aside what they want in the service and defense of others. *Sheepdogs Among the Flock* gives us a front row seat to learn from the best. A must-read for every pastor, every leader, and every layperson.

Pastor Michael Phillips
Kingdom Life Church
Baltimore, Maryland

Every pastor who has successfully built a strong, significant and soul-winning ministry has been surrounded by anointed helpers—men and women of great character, caliber and capacity. Elder Canfield, as I respectfully and affectionately know him, is both an example and an embodiment of this ideal. Filled with the Holy Spirit and wisdom, rooted in integrity, and clothed with humility, Elder Canfield has written *Sheepdogs Among the Flock* as a tool to empower others who are anointed to assist their pastors to honorably take their stand and serve alongside their pastor for the advancement of the Kingdom. This well-written work will stir the hearts and strengthen the hands of those called to serve a vision greater than their own to the end that God's Church will be edified, Jesus will be exalted, and His Kingdom will be expanded. I cannot wait to share it with our staff!

Bishop R.J. Matthews
Kingdom International Church
Columbus, Mississippi

There is no one that I know of who is better qualified to write on the subject of serving pastors and people than Elder Bill Canfield—no one. I have known Bill for 30 years and have watched him serve his pastor and congregation with complete dedication and heart that entire time.

Serving in a number two position for many years may seem to some like a second-rate career. But Bill would argue that assumption and state that the "*get me to the top as fast as possible*" mentality has ravaged the church and left the sheep stranded and bleeding. That is why I am so excited about this book. It is a must-read for anyone wanting to live a life of purpose and influence.

Pastor Gary Keesee
Faith Life Church
New Albany, Ohio

Sheepdogs Among the Flock
The Art of Assisting Your Pastor

Published by:
Canfield Communication
Canfieldcommunication.com
Billandpaulacanfield.com

Typesetting by: Palmer Enterprises
Cover Art by: Cameron Fontana

Unless otherwise noted, all Scripture references are from the Modern English Version of the Bible. Copyright © 2014 by Military Bible Association. Used by permission. All rights reserved.

Contents

FOREWORD

My pastor and mentor of fifteen years, Dr. Lester Sumrall, told me, "If you leave this earth with two or three true friends, you've died a rich man." When Dr. Sumrall went to receive his eternal reward, that pastoral void was filled by not only an admired and respected mentor, but by one of those very few true friends.

Elder Bill Canfield, as we know him here at World Harvest Church, serves not only as the Senior Elder of a ministry that's touching the world with the Gospel, but also as my family's pastor. He is a true man of God who speaks into our lives, watches over us and covers us in prayer every day, and we love him with all of our hearts. He is a man of unwavering integrity, impeccable character and keen spiritual insight. He is a well of wisdom and our resident theologian.

Elder Canfield has not just written another book about ministry. He has provided a God-inspired roadmap for everyone who has a heart to hold up the arms of their own pastor. Bill refers to himself in the following pages as being like a sheepdog—helping the shepherd with the sheep. And help me he has! Going on four decades now, he has been unwaveringly faithful to his calling, always ready in and out of season with an encouraging word, a helping hand and an anointing to accomplish the task at hand.

Now in the third stage of his life, the giving years, every page has been penned for one purpose: to pass on the insights that he has learned—inspired by the trials and triumphs on the front lines of gospel ministry with me as my trusted pastor, helper and friend—to a new generation.

It is my deepest prayer that his book will inspire you to make every effort to imitate his faith and follow in his footsteps.

Dr. Rod Parsley
Columbus, Ohio

ACKNOWLEDGEMENTS

Authors generally get credit for the books they write, and in some cases, they deserve it. Any recognition I receive for this book must be shared with many others, without whose input it would have never been possible.

Without an understanding and supportive wife and family, no married man can really achieve success, either in ministry or any other endeavor. My wife, Paula, and our children, Erin, Julia and Jordan, have been the best family a man could ever have. I especially appreciate my longsuffering wife's efforts to improve this book in countless ways.

The laboratory where I have learned most of what I know about ministry has been the main campus of World Harvest Church, in Columbus, Ohio, where Dr. Rod Parsley and his family have allowed me to help for over thirty-five years. It is an inestimable privilege to be able to serve this great man of God, and God's people, in this local church.

Some of the most significant things I have learned about ministry have come from observing the lives of my fellow elders and their wives, as well as the staff at the church.

I also owe a great debt of gratitude to all the marvelous ministry gifts who have made such a remarkable impact on my life, as well as the thousands of believers who have influenced me in ways I am still only beginning to understand.

I must also thank a teacher in the truest sense of the word, Dr. Candice Thomas-Maddox, without whose encouragement this work would have died in infancy.

Finally, to all the students I have had the privilege of instructing at Valor Christian College, I can say without fear of contradiction that it is the teacher who learns more than the student.

William C. Canfield
Canal Winchester. Ohio

i

INTRODUCTION

Someone approached a friend of mine with a question about his role in his church. "Are you one of the pastors?" they asked.

"No," my friend replied, "we only have one pastor here."

"So, you don't consider yourself a shepherd?"

"No, I'm not called to be a shepherd," my friend said.

"Well, if you're not a shepherd, what are you?"

"I'm a sheepdog. I help the shepherd with the sheep."

This exchange helped me immensely, because I didn't find my calling neatly categorized and outlined in the traditional five-fold ministry gift offices listed in Ephesians 4. I know I am a teacher in the body of Christ, but that doesn't encompass all I believe I am called to do.

Even though *sheepdog* is not one of the gifts mentioned by name, I believe it encapsulates the intention and gifting of many men and women who are devoted to the well-being of the sheep. This could properly be described as the ministry of helps. But to me, there is something satisfying in identifying with the role of a faithful sheepdog, assisting the shepherd in whatever way he needs it, using the skills and abilities God gave me.

Pastors are under a lot of pressure these days in our postmodern, increasingly secular culture. There are many men and women who are called to help shepherds, but they may need a word of encouragement to step into their assigned role. This book is meant to offer that encouragement.

I am convinced that one of the best ways to help pastors is to help those who have been called to stand with them. This book is filled with insights I have gained from over thirty-five years of full-time ministry service as someone called alongside to help a pastor.

The time is long past that we can afford to expect only those on the platform or with a microphone to do all the work of the ministry. Paul made it clear in Ephesians 4 that the five-fold ministry gift offices were for the perfecting of the saints, so the saints could do the work of the ministry. I trust this book will be received as a worthwhile contribution toward moving the work of the saints forward.

2 Corinthians 8:12 says:

> *For if there is a willing mind first, the gift is accepted according to what a man possesses and not according to what he does not possess.*

My prayer is that this offering is an acceptable one.

CHAPTER 1

Help Not Just Wanted, But Needed

The pastor cried out, "God, I can't take it anymore! I can't take it, and it's driving me crazy. I just want it to be over. God, I want you to kill me!" It was a declaration born of desperation.

This pastor was leading a church that had grown almost overnight to incalculable proportions. He was a remarkably gifted and powerfully anointed minster, but the pressures and problems of pastoring so many people had become too much for one man to handle.

When it looked as though no help was forthcoming and no end was in sight, the overwhelmed pastor—without hope and without options—asked God to bring his life to a swift and merciful conclusion.

Instead, God brought Pastor Moses the help he needed to fulfill his calling. And God will bring your pastor the help he needs to fulfill his calling as well. The help your pastor needs could be you.

Sheepdogs Among the Flock

CRISIS AMONG THE CLERGY

The children of Israel in the book of Exodus were making history. They didn't realize it, because they were too focused on finishing the necessary preparations for their departure. All they could know for sure was that they were leaving—anticipating a life free from the drudgery and hopelessness that was all they and the generations before them had known.

Some of them were excited about a new adventure. Some were cautiously optimistic. Others were frightened, because they were leaving everything that was familiar. Still others were antagonistic, since there were so many unanswered questions. What would happen to them now? Where would they find the resources to sustain themselves? They didn't even know where they were going—and what's more, they were packing up in the middle of the night. Why the need for such haste?

Of course, when we look back at the Exodus story, we don't generally think of it in these terms. We read it as a historical account of an event that happened thousands of years ago, that was unprecedented in any age before or since. But we tend to forget this is a story that involved real people, who had real requirements for everyday survival. They needed food for their children and themselves. Their livestock consumed tremendous quantities of pasture and water. They couldn't travel any faster than the least of them could walk. It was, by any measure, a monumental undertaking.

Help Not Just Wanted, But Needed

There is no doubt that God gave them supernatural help, but He didn't just snap His fingers and place them in the Promised Land. They had to get there by overcoming natural barriers, desert conditions and hostile adversaries. And the responsibility of shepherding them all the way to their destination ultimately belonged to one man.

Moses is often referred to as the first example of a pastor in the Bible, since he was the one tasked with looking after the needs of this enormous and multifaceted flock on the way to Canaan. God never intended for His people to go straight to the Promised Land, because He had some instructions He needed to give them first—so the first stop was at Sinai.

It was at the foot of Mount Sinai that God gave His people the law, and instructed them how to build the tabernacle, anoint the priesthood and organize themselves into divisions for efficient travel. These precautions were necessary to make their trip not just more convenient, but possible. They weren't ready until more than a year of preparation had passed.

It was only then that they set out to possess their land of promise. It only took a few days after they left their yearlong encampment for the complaining to begin.

The story of Israel's escape from Egyptian captivity is not only a historically accurate record of actual events, but an example of the kinds of victories and challenges that await every local body of believers. All the fundamental elements are there—Moses is the pastor, the Israelites are the flock, the Promised Land is the ultimate destination, and the journey is the life and the circumstances we are in right now.

The Israelites' first point of contention was that they were tired of manna—that miraculous substance that God had given them every morning since their departure from Egypt. By now, they had fixed it in every way they could, and they wanted something new. The grumbling and murmuring became so widespread and troublesome that Moses cried out to God in Numbers 11:11-15:

> *Why have You hurt Your servant? And why have I not found favor in Your eyes, that You lay the burden of all this people on me? Have I conceived all this people? Have I given them birth, that You should say to me, 'Carry them in your bosom, as a nurse bears the nursing child,' to the land which You swore to their fathers? Where am I to get meat to give to all these people? For they weep to me, saying, 'Give us meat, that we may eat.' I am not able to bear all these people alone, because the burden is too heavy for me. If You do this to me, please kill me at once, if I have found favor in Your eyes, and do not let me see my misery.*

You may not have heard your pastor say these words publicly, but if he's been in pastoral ministry very long, he has surely said them, or at least thought them, privately.

Moses needed help with his people, and your pastor needs help with his people, as well. God's answer for Moses was to anoint others to help him. God's answer for your pastor is exactly the same—He will anoint other people to help him. God is looking for someone to help your pastor. And that someone might just be you.

Your obedience can provide a source of strength and encouragement to a pastor who is on the brink of spiritual or emotional disaster. Accepting God's call to help can be the difference that turns the failure of a church's mission to reach its community and the world into a resounding success.

Taken as a group, there is a crisis among the clergy. Lots of new churches are starting, but many others are closing. Pastors are, for the most part, genuinely committed to their calling, but are often unsatisfied with their circumstances. Discouragement and discontent among ministers is common. In many cases, hours are long, salaries are low, rewards are inconsistent, and satisfaction remains elusive. What can be done to reverse this state of affairs?

HELP IS ON THE WAY

I don't have all the answers, but I see from the Word of God that one of the answers is me—and you, too. God is raising up an army of helpers from among the ranks of believers who will obey their calling to help just as much as pastors will obey their calling to lead.

The first example of this in the life and ministry of Moses is recorded in Exodus 18, when Jethro, Moses' father-in-law, gave him good advice about assigning administrators to help him deal with the everyday controversies that arose among God's people.

There are two benefits that accrued immediately. In Exodus 18:18, Jethro warned Moses of what would happen if Moses did all the work himself:

You will surely wear yourself out, both you, and these people who are with you, for this thing is too heavy for you. You are not able to do it by yourself.

This is as good a description as I have heard of some pastors who either have no help, or in some cases, will accept no help. They literally and figuratively wear themselves out, as well as all those around them. God brought Moses help to prevent this from happening.

The other benefit is found in Exodus 18:25-26:

Moses chose capable men out of all Israel and made them heads over the people, rulers of thousands, rulers of hundreds, rulers of fifties, and rulers of tens. They judged the people at all times. They brought the difficult cases to Moses, but they judged every small matter themselves.

Other capable men used their administrative abilities to assist Moses in keeping the camp of Israel running smoothly. This not only helped Moses, but also helped the men who were helping by allowing them to use an ability they had obviously been given. Of course, it also helped the people by resolving their issues quickly and with a minimum of disruption.

Help Not Just Wanted, But Needed

Not everyone who thinks they need to see the pastor of a church really does. Every local church, regardless of how small the congregation is, should have someone in its midst who is capable enough to provide a word of encouragement, an appropriate passage of Scripture, or an anointed prayer to help someone in a time of need. It doesn't have to be a staff member or a person who graduated from Bible school—but it does need to be someone who has a heart to help others.

In Numbers 11, God's answer to Moses' cry of desperation involved taking some of the anointing that was on Moses and placing it on seventy elders who would help Moses bear the burden he was assigned to carry. We aren't told exactly how they did that. It may be that their responsibility was to reinforce and remind everyone in the camp of the instructions that came from God through Moses. Whatever their role, we know they received the same spirit that was in Moses. The evidence was that they began to prophesy on that occasion, so that all those present could see that they had been set apart for their assigned task.

This does not mean that they became prophets, nor did it mean they had a position equal to Moses. It means that whenever God assigns someone to help, He is faithful to give them the equipment necessary to fulfill their assignment. It may not be the same measure or degree of enabling that is given to a pastor or other leader, but it is valuable nevertheless. We know that it is, because it came from God, and we should consider anything from His hand as valuable.

These men did not become Moses' counselors, expecting Moses to do what they said. Moses still received his instructions from God. Those who serve in a subordinate role are not in a position to tell a pastor what he should or should not do. There may be occasions when it is all right to offer opinions (usually when the pastor asks for them), but most of the time, they should be content to follow directions without offering opinions. You give instruction to those below you, not to those above you.

When it comes to approaching God, He accepts us all on the same basis. We are all worshippers before His throne. But in the administration of His kingdom, there is an order of authority that is prescribed by God and needs to be followed. The head of the church is the Lord Jesus Christ. The head of a local church is a pastor. He may have another title, but that is his function—to lead, to feed and to meet the need.

Those who help a pastor should understand where they stand—which is under his direction, not over him. If they try to be over the pastor, it means that they are trying to insert themselves between the pastor and God. That is not where a helper should be. That is the place that Jesus Christ has reserved for Himself. Stay out of His way.

I heard a seasoned minister describe it this way: "Can you imagine what would have happened if Moses had listened to the advice of all those seventy elders? They would still be walking around in the wilderness."[1] If everyone is in charge, no one makes much progress. God does not run His kingdom by the vote of a committee. He intends His church to follow one vision from one leader. Anything with more than one head is a monster, and God doesn't ordain monsters.

Shepherds can listen to what the sheepdogs are telling them about the condition of the sheep, but they must make decisions regarding what to do about it based on what God tells them. Shepherds don't get advice, direction and correction from the sheepdogs, nor do they get it from the sheep. That would result in chaos.

Shepherds should be attentive to hear the sheep when there is a problem, and astute shepherds will even learn things about the care and protection of the flock from observing those they shepherd, but the pastor has a higher authority to whom he reports.

However, there are ways that a pastor can sabotage the effectiveness of those God brings to help him. Some of them have to do with his attitude toward, or treatment of those people.

MANAGEMENT ISSUES

Many pastors are good managers—they have to be, since they oversee every aspect of the church's functions. A pastor has done just about everything that can be done in a local church and is familiar with how everything operates. He is relieved when he can delegate responsibility in a certain area to a helper. The helper attempts to do what he has been directed to do, sometimes with varying degrees of success.

Conflict sometimes arises, and one of the reasons is that the pastor may have a very specific understanding about not only *what* needs done, but *how* it needs to be done. Whether the helper shares this understanding is another matter. This may result in the helper either being interrupted from accomplishing their task or being replaced altogether—by the pastor.

This process is called *micromanagement,* and it can be devastating for the pastor, the helper and the church. Delegation is more art than science, but it is important to give clear instructions, then allow someone the time and space to get the job done. Nobody will do things exactly the way someone else does them, because every individual is unique.

If helpers feel that they can't successfully meet a leader's expectations, one of two things will happen: either nobody will step forward to do anything, since they know it is likely to result in disapproval, or a helper who began—but wasn't allowed to finish—will become offended. In either case, the pastor must do the job himself, and he is right back where he started, but many times with an offended helper (or a suddenly unavailable potential helper) as a consequence.

Another problem can happen when pastors or leaders withhold the things from their helpers that are necessary for success. The things that are most often withheld are affirmation, information, opportunity, and money.

Help Not Just Wanted, But Needed

One of the most significant needs a helper has is to receive affirmation that they are doing a good job. Many pastors understand that they don't preach for the praise of men, and they don't measure their success by whether or not they obtain it. But many sheepdogs need the affirmation of those over them, and when they don't get it, it may cause them to become negatively introspective and depressed.

While lack of praise is debilitating, public rebuke is deadly. Nothing will damage a sheepdog more quickly or more seriously, and nothing will destroy a relationship between a leader and a helper more completely. Here is the operative principle that should always be followed: praise in public, correct in private. The benefits are worth the self-control that is needed to follow this procedure.

A visiting minister raised his voice in rebuke to one of his assistants while both were on the platform during a service. The assistant left that ministry shortly afterward. Another well-known evangelist threw something at his own sound technician during a large event. That helper, too, soon found another place to serve.

Accurate and timely information is the currency of success in any collaborative effort, and ministry is no exception. Failure to properly expedite projects large or small is usually the result of a communication breakdown. Followers accomplish tasks properly by having information, not intuition. If a leader does not give a helper the right information, they will not be able to produce the expected result.

Sheepdogs Among the Flock

Generally speaking, faithful service in one area should result in doors of opportunity opening in other areas. If a pastor or leader denies their helpers the genuine opportunities for advancement their conscientious service may bring to them, it can cause great loss to the body of Christ.

One of my instructors in Bible college started out with a job duplicating cassette tapes in that ministry, but because he seriously and thoroughly devoted himself to the study of the Bible, he eventually had the chance to teach a class as a substitute. He later became one of the most respected and influential instructors at the school. Another man was confident he heard the call of God upon his life to teach the Bible, but he was a college student at the time. He was also one of the pilots for the school's president. He later developed a world-renowned ministry of his own.

Many people who have served on the staff of World Harvest Church have gone on to begin successful ministries and churches. Their success was expedited by a door of opportunity being opened by Pastor Parsley.

Money is another area that can cause problems between a pastor or other leader and his helpers. There is an old witticism about the sentiment of board members or church members toward their pastor: "Lord, you keep him humble, and we'll keep him poor." If the same attitude prevails from church members, church leaders or the pastor toward the helpers who are part of the paid staff, they will get what they pay for—which is not much.

Help Not Just Wanted, But Needed

Pride and arrogance can also cause a rock of offense when it comes from a pastor toward his helpers. I have heard of churches where a youth group or Sunday school class became larger than the congregation in the worship service. It takes a rare pastor to celebrate this success instead of trying to stop it.

On other occasions, I knew of men who were hired as assistants who ended up doing everything in the church — and I mean *everything*—except, of course, preaching. The pastor only came to preach, and even then, showed up late and left early, and had little interaction with the church members. This state of affairs did not last very long — at least not for those helpers, because they quickly figured out that doing all of the work and receiving none of the reward was not a winning formula — at least, not for them.

We had a guest (only once — he was never invited to return) who verbally attacked his assistant in front of others because the assistant didn't inspect the restroom before the guest used it. This was a spotless private restroom, not one that was available to the public.

This kind of attitude may prevail in the world, but believers should never engage in it. This is God's kingdom, not man's. Oversights should be overlooked, not made the cause for character assassination. Leaders should never despise their helpers — they are gifts from God that can multiply their effectiveness.

I was with a leader who was picking up a world-renowned ministry guest at the airport. We had arranged to take him to dinner. As we were getting out of the vehicle on our way into the restaurant, I noticed the leader's credit card, which he had inadvertently left on the vehicle's console. I knew we would need it, so I put it in my pocket. When the time came to pay the check, the leader began patting his pockets searching for the card. I remembered that I had it, and showed it to him.

"I found it in the van," I said. The look of relief on his face was a great thing to see.

"Thank you," he said, and never were words more genuine. It was a very fulfilling feeling to know that I was able to fill in a gap in such a small but significant way.

Leaders need helpers, and helpers need leaders. Let's work together to accomplish God's will.

CHAPTER 2

What Happens in the Fold Stays in the Fold

When I was a kid, one of my favorite cartoons was about a sheepdog that would guard a flock of sheep from any threat—most commonly a gaunt and flea-bitten wolf. The wolf would spend all day hatching some misbegotten plot to make off with one of the oblivious sheep, and the sheepdog would inevitably get the best of the would-be predator and pound the stuffing out of it.

At the end of their shift, both the dog and the wolf would appear at a time clock hanging on a tree, punch their time cards, greet each other amiably and call it a day. I thought it was hilarious.

My life's work has convinced me, though, that there is nothing funny about the wolf's desire to ravage the sheep, and there is no room for anything but enmity between the guardians of the flock and the enemies of the flock. However, the point of the last scene of the cartoon was that regardless of what goes on at the office, there is no need to take your work home with you.

YOU CAN'T WORK 24/7

I remember hearing an experienced minister respond to a question about how to keep difficulties in the ministry from affecting life at home. He said:

"When I came out of the church office at 5:00 p.m. and closed the door, I left all the problems of the ministry inside. If a problem tried to sneak out, I just kicked it in the behind and said, 'Get back in there. You don't go anywhere. You stay here. I'll be back tomorrow morning to take care of you.'"[2]

I realize that ministry doesn't exist only between eight and five, and that you can't schedule every ministry need so that it doesn't conflict with other plans you have made. People don't generally have crises at convenient times, and if you have no heart to meet the need when the need is urgent, you should probably be doing something else. If you are in ministry any length of time at all, there will be times when you need to do ministry work on holidays, birthdays, vacations, anniversaries or other special occasions.

But there will be other times when you need to put aside the *"care of all the churches,"* as Paul put it in 2 Corinthians 11:28, and reserve a day to do something with your family or your spouse, stay home by yourself or go somewhere to do something that helps you recharge and be refreshed.

Refusing to take time for yourself is problematic, since it is contrary to the God-given instruction that we ought to take one day per week to rest. It's amazing to me that ministers tell other people to take a break to worship God on Sunday, yet they work nearly every Sunday of their lives.

Many of them take another day off (often Monday) to make up for it, which is not a bad idea. But since those involved in the care of the sheep are on call all the time—and if they are senior pastors they are eventually responsible for everything in the local church—they may have a day off in name, but not in fact.

I'm not suggesting that we should not work hard at what we do. The forty-hour work week is a relatively recent phenomenon and was not developed for ministers of the gospel. I believe that kingdom work is a full-time occupation and deserves our very best effort. But when I hear of ministers routinely working from dawn to midnight for weeks at a time, I shake my head in disbelief. Adjustments need to be made before disaster happens.

There are those times when sacrifices need to be made by everyone in order to make something extraordinary happen, to overcome an unusual or unforeseen challenge, or to make a special meeting come together. But nobody can live happily very long moving perpetually from one crisis to another.

Sheepdogs Among the Flock

This points out a danger that everyone who is conscientious about ministry faces at some time. It is easy to confuse your work *for* God and your relationship *with* God, but they are not the same. Too often, a minister justifies additional effort since he is doing it for the kingdom of God. But God is not automatically pleased with more and more effort, especially if it is attempting to accomplish something He has not ordained.

I look at it this way: if I were never able to do anything else for Him, I would still have a relationship with Him. If I could never teach another Bible lesson or do any of the other things that I have done in ministry, I would still love God and serve Him to the best of my ability.

My relationship with God does not depend on what I do—it depends on who He is, and who I am in relationship to Him. Of course, I want to do a good job at what He has called and anointed me to do, but He loved me and died for me before I ever did a thing for Him. All the things I have done and all that I could ever do could not get Him to love me more than He does now; if I never did another thing for Him, He would love me no less.

If our relationship with God is based on our performance, we will find ourselves continually discouraged and defeated. There are always things about our performance that will not meet our expectations or the expectations of others. God wants us to do things for Him—and do them with a spirit of excellence—but His relationship with us goes far beyond the things we can do. Our work for God is *because* of His love for us, not to try to *earn* His love. This is a fundamental principle of the Word of God that needs to be recovered in our lives.

Another issue that arises when ministers (and even volunteers) find themselves overcommitted is family problems. Spouses and children are generally very understanding and accommodating to the call of God on a person's life, but there are times when other things must be set aside so you can minister to your own family.

I enjoyed playing baseball as a youngster, and always expected I would have the chance to involve my son in the sport as well. Imagine my surprise when we celebrated my son's tenth birthday and he still did not know how to play baseball. We were in the back yard trying to play catch, and I realized that he had not learned the fundamentals of the game. I thought that was really strange until I realized I was the one who should have been teaching him!

That was a serious wake-up call, and I knew I had to make some adjustments right away. After all, someone else could look after church business, but I was the only one who could be a dad to my son. I am convinced this perspective needs to be regained by many dads and moms in the ministry.

I have seen some children raised in preachers' homes who end up despising the church, detesting the ministry and even hating God because they think God and the church are to blame for their parents' absence. If we are going to be examples to the flock, it doesn't make sense that we should help strengthen other families and weaken our own.

Sometimes it can be easier for a minister to say *yes* to every ministry need or opportunity, even when doing so means he must say *no* to his own family. Ministers can be highly creative at coming up with all kinds of justifications for doing this—after all, they are fulfilling their calling, or ministering to the people God gave them, or making additional income—the list goes on and on.

Those rationalizations will seem ridiculous in subsequent years when the children are gone from home and irreplaceable opportunities for fellowship, interaction, loving and bonding are lost forever. An old adage affirms that no man ever died regretting spending too much time with his family.

PRIVACY PROBLEMS

Another issue that causes difficulties in ministry families occurs when problems from the church come into the home. Most preachers I know consider their homes to be a refuge from the madness that sometimes characterizes ministry. In some places, though, the parsonage is still next door to the church. This is unfortunate, because in this scenario the pastor and his family never have an opportunity to be free from the continual interruptions by people who come to the church during odd hours for a variety of reasons.

I firmly believe ministers should not talk about certain ministry issues at home. I don't mean that you can never tell others in your family what you did at work that day, but problems that arise among God's people should not be discussed outside the office. There are certain things about which you can confide in your spouse, but due to their confidential nature, many things should never be mentioned.

You want your spouse and children to think you have the greatest occupation in the world, and that the people you serve are the best people on earth. This doesn't mean you should be unrealistically cheerful all the time, but there is no reason to burden your family with all the situations you deal with in ministry.

Preachers have different views about giving people access to their private telephone numbers or their homes. How you feel about this is probably directly related to the number of people you serve, and to a certain extent, what kind of personality you have.

Some people make it a point not to give out their phone number. This is fine as long as someone knows how to get in touch with you in the event of an emergency. I remember one occasion when I did not receive any information about a family who called the church late one Friday evening to request that I be involved in an upcoming funeral. This was mainly because of assumptions on the part of others who could have made sure I received the information.

One of the assumptions was that my home number would not be available, which proves that sometimes the best way to hide something is to leave it in plain sight. In this case, much embarrassment could have been avoided by a casual glance through the telephone directory (of course, this was before the advent of cell phones).

On other occasions, I have had people take advantage of my availability, and try to call at all hours to discuss things that did not qualify as emergencies. Of course, what qualifies as an emergency will differ depending on what the emergency is and who is having it! A lady called me at home one evening and was extremely upset about an incident that had happened many years before.

I explained as patiently as I could that if it had not been resolved for that long, waiting until the next day would not cause additional problems. Of course, if someone has died or is critically ill, then ministry is needed right away.

Technology has made it much easier to deal with the phone. Features such as voice mail, caller ID and the like eliminate the need to take every call the moment the phone rings. In years past, answering the telephone was a big deal—family members actually competed with each other to see who could get to the phone to answer it first.

Now people are likely to let it ring, find out who left a message and decide if it warrants a return call. And now there is text messaging, which in many cases is replacing voice communication altogether.

I am nearly equally amused and appalled by cell phones. They have become indispensable tools (or toys) for most people, and I seem to be one of the few dinosaurs who looks for a reason not to carry one. In my experience, cell phones work great—except when they don't, whether due to an area with no cellular service, the battery being discharged or some other problem that occurs at the most inopportune moment. The likelihood of your cell phone malfunctioning often seems to be in direct proportion to the urgency or importance of your need to communicate effectively.

And now, the proliferation of social media provides any number of other ways to get in touch with someone—so many, in fact, it is often difficult to remember to check every one of them every day.

It is amazing to me that we have more means of communication than ever before, and we still can't seem to get in touch with anyone!

It is another matter to have people come to your home uninvited. If the parsonage is next to the church, unannounced visitors will be inevitable. (Most support staff, however, do not live on church property, so this is rarely a problem for sheepdogs.) Many ministers value their privacy, and even more so if they have very little time at home, so uninvited guests can be problematic. Some people are more gregarious than others, and like to be around people all the time, day and night.

The Bible instructs us to be given to hospitality, and this is really not as difficult as it sounds. There is something fundamentally wrong if you can never open your home to those who visit or stop by. You don't have to have the best house in the finest neighborhood to be friendly, and you don't have to feed visitors a six-course meal to be hospitable. But our efforts at hospitality should never infringe on our responsibilities to our own families. In any case, there needs to be agreement among family members about how these kinds of things will be handled, and a plan of action to follow in the event of genuine emergencies.

A friend of mine was involved in street ministry, which involved regular interaction with people in difficult and sometimes dangerous lifestyles. In an effort to reach out to those in his community, he opened his home to those to whom he ministered. He explained all this to his wife, who said she understood. One night when my friend was out the doorbell rang. When his wife opened the door, a man fell bleeding and unconscious across the threshold into her unsuspecting arms. She managed to catch him, lower him to the floor and begin some necessary first aid. Her husband later complimented her on what he considered a truly heroic response (even though it may have been more out of reflex than compassion), since many wives might have been so shocked they would have jumped back screaming and let the victim fall on his face on the foyer floor.

YOU NEED A CONFIDANT

It is important for every minister to find someone in whom they can confide about things involving ministry. These people should only be those you can trust implicitly, and they should never be the people you serve. At times, even your peers cannot fulfill this need, and you will be compelled to seek out someone you can trust beyond your ordinary circle of influence. This may be a ministry colleague in another city or state, or a mentor or person who has had more experience in ministry who can provide a listening ear or wise counsel during a time of challenge or crisis.

There will be times when the best person for you to talk to will be your pastor. It is not necessary for you to make the pastor you serve aware of every sniffle that affects you and your family, but you should trust him enough to share major areas of concern with him.

If you don't trust him enough to do that, you need to seriously evaluate your relationship with him. Time after time I have been spared from making bad decisions by the anointed input of my pastor. Most of the time, my biggest regret was not talking to him sooner.

If you find yourself conflicted about your responsibilities in God's house, it is important to know how much you can or should share about your concerns with your spouse. A wife who is conscientious about her husband's well-being may do her best to move him away from the things that he indicates are troubling him. She will do all kinds of things, either consciously or subconsciously, to get him away from a difficult job situation, sabotaging his efforts to resolve it without even realizing what she is doing.

If the spouse is a husband, he may feel the need to fix whatever is troubling his wife as a means of protecting her from real or perceived harm. Either of these scenarios can have harmful consequences since it will usually involve a hasty and emotional response rather than a patient and reasoned one.

The ideal ministry mate will love what you do. At the very least, your spouse cannot be hostile to your calling and the responsibilities it entails and should not be lukewarm or neutral. The kinds of sacrifices that are necessary to be effective in ministry require support at home. If it is not forthcoming, it will be very difficult for you to give maximum effort to the work of the gospel. There is nothing as damaging as a spouse who does not understand or support ministry work, and nothing as helpful and encouraging as one who does.

When I first acknowledged the call to ministry, my wife and I and our two-year-old twin daughters were living in a little house in an older neighborhood. We were so poor that poor people felt sorry for us, and I had little clear direction about what to do with the call on my life. We had a good local church home, a wonderful pastor and faithful friends who were older in the Lord and who were willing to disciple us.

During this time, I had the opportunity to accompany my pastor and an evangelist as they traveled to several church revival meetings. These were eye-opening experiences and helped to solidify my intention to obey God in pursuit of my call to ministry. During one of these trips to another state, I discovered that I had taken the keys to our car with me. Since we had recently lost the other set of keys, this left my wife without any way to drive.

To make matters worse, we were not at home when I left, meaning that she was stranded away from home, and had to arrange for friends to take her and our children back to our house. I felt terrible and was sure that the result of this would be to make my wife hate me and hate the ministry for putting her at such risk. This was in the days before cell phones, so I was unable to call to see how she was faring while I was gone.

When I finally arrived at home late one night, I feared the worst. The girls were in bed, and Paula was waiting for my arrival. But instead of telling me what an irresponsible husband I was by putting her in such a difficult position — no money, no car and no plan — she smiled and showed me an apple pie she had baked to celebrate my coming home after being involved in ministry. Someone had given her the apples (we had no money to buy them) and she did that because she wanted me to know that she supported me. I knew then that I could do anything or become anything God called me to do or become with this woman by my side. I pray that every person involved in ministry would be so blessed.

CHAPTER 3

Mrs., Ministry and Money

A ny disclaimer about this chapter may be too late, since those who are gender sensitive may already be upset at what they may suspect are sexist assumptions. Let's face it, though: even though great strides have been made in the past forty years, ministry in many cultures is still predominantly a men's club. It's my purpose to speak to the often unseen and unnoticed needs and conflicts that occur in the hearts and lives of those who are ministry spouses.

While I am making disclaimers, let me say that I do believe that women can be called to and anointed for full-time ministry. Even if you are convinced otherwise, I still have some things to share that will be helpful to you. I also need to mention that many times I use masculine personal pronouns to refer to both men and women. My reason for doing so is to simplify the communication process, not to deny women their rightful place in God's kingdom.

Sheepdogs Among the Flock

MARRIED AND IN THE MINISTRY

I believe that any call to ministry a married person receives also involves their spouse. The kind of involvement necessary to be successful in ministry makes a supportive and understanding marriage partner not just a convenience, but a necessity. If you are currently involved in ministry, or contemplating becoming involved in ministry, and are considering being married, make sure that any potential mate is aware of the demands peculiar to that occupation. If they are pulling the other direction, or are even indifferent, the results will be devastating.

I have known more than one minister who failed to fulfill their calling because of a spouse who did not understand the needs or priorities that are involved in ministry. I have also known of marriages that failed because a spouse was not in agreement with the call of God on their mate's life. The right marriage partner will multiply your effectiveness in ministry. The wrong one will either diminish it or end it.

This does not mean you can neglect your supportive and helpful spouse while you go everywhere else in the world and minister to the multitudes. If you are married, your marriage is more important than your ministry. Let me say that again: if you are married, your marriage is more important than your ministry. What kind of testimony is it if you are powerfully anointed when ministering to the masses, but a mess when it comes to blessing your own spouse?

I heard this illustrated by a story about an old fisherman. He spent a lot of time on the water, and his wife was unhappy that he was gone from home for such prolonged periods of time. He suggested that she become involved in a hobby that would keep her occupied while he was away. After some discussion, they decided that she would try raising chickens. She didn't know much about them, but she was willing to learn.

The next time the old salt headed out to sea, his wife went to town and bought some likely-looking chickens. When he returned home, he was pleased to see chickens in the yard, but his wife was still unhappy. Even though she had a nice flock of chickens, she didn't understand why she didn't have any chicks. Her husband pointed out that she wasn't ever going to have any little chickens without a rooster. Soon he was gone again, and when he returned he found not one, but two roosters in the yard.

"My dear," the fisherman said, "you can't have two roosters in the same henhouse."

His wife said, "You can when one is fishing all the time."

Unfortunately, there have been ministers who have become so wrapped up in their ministry that they haven't paid attention to what was happening in the henhouse, and divorces took place that could have been avoided.

I suspect that far more often, spouses have long-standing bitterness or resentment about feeling left out after having sacrificed their dreams to support someone else's success. The undercurrents of such resentments can have far-reaching implications, even though the spouses who harbor them may not verbalize or even acknowledge their sentiments for years.

We must keep our priorities straight in this matter. I have heard of (and from) many whose spouses were involved in ministry and were desperate for prayer for their families and homes. Some of them were well-known.

Winning the world is an honorable goal, but don't allow your marriage and family to be compromised in the process. It's worth whatever effort is necessary to keep the devil from destroying your home.

Here's something that should go without saying, but it obviously needs to be said, since so many ministers still fall prey to it: don't allow yourself to be alone with someone of the opposite sex, unless you are related to them. If you do, you're practically handing the devil an open invitation to ruin your ministry and your marriage. I have known of several men in ministry whose reputations and marriage relationships have been shredded because of their refusal to recognize the impropriety of an unguarded ministry relationship with a woman. In each case, it led to intimacy, which resulted in unnecessary and protracted pain.

One of the best ways to avoid this kind of temptation is to simply refuse to be alone with someone of the opposite sex who is not your spouse (or mother, daughter or sister). This includes personal ministry, riding in a car, having personal meetings in offices (even about church business), going to lunch or anything else that would put you in a compromised position. Any inconvenience these restrictions cause will be miniscule compared to the problems that will arise from falling prey to sexual temptation.

Another thing ministers need be cautious about is developing close friendships with anyone in the church. This is especially important for those in support ministries, and even more crucial for their spouses. Sometimes friendships involve sharing confidences, and that can breed disaster, especially if the friend is not very discreet. This creates problems for men and women, but it seems especially difficult for wives whose husbands support pastors. Quite often, they have no opportunity to meet people in similar positions, and so have nobody in whom they can confide. If they share their struggles with someone in the church and that person talks about their conversations, many misunderstandings and problems can result.

When this is combined with a spouse who is gone or distracted most of the time, the wife feels left out, and may become angry or resentful. These feelings may not be admitted or even recognized, especially at first, but a neglected spouse may come to the point where they do not celebrate or even appreciate any success that comes as a result of the ministry of their spouse. This leads to all kinds of trouble at home, even to the point where the offended spouse may unconsciously try to sabotage the efforts of their spouse or the ministry to which they are attached. There are any number of symptoms that indicate this may be happening, among which are being critical, withdrawing from involvement or even engaging in behavior contrary to a Christian testimony.

GOOD...FOR NOTHING

Another problem sometimes arises that is peculiar to wives of those in ministry. Because people know her spouse is in a position of responsibility in the church, they may try to get close to her, not because they are interested in any kind of friendship, but because they think she will be a ready source of all kinds of juicy church gossip. If she supplies that kind of information, the "friends" will amplify it and carry it to the ends of the earth, creating various divisions and other mayhem. If she doesn't or won't dish the dirt, the "friends" will quickly move on to some other potential source, leaving her feeling used.

This brings up a question: what is the wife of a minister good for? Much of the time, she will answer: "My husband gets paid to be good, but I'm expected to be good for nothing."

Sometimes churches consider a staff member's wife to be an extra employee. This problem is most acute for pastor's wives, who are often pressed into service as the church administrator, praise and worship leader, organist, pianist, Sunday school overseer, women's group leader, bookkeeper, cleaning lady and who knows what else. What is worse, most of the time she does not get paid, either in money or in recognition. Here are the questions that should be asked: what can she do, what does she want to do and, most importantly, what is she called to do?

It is important for everyone in a local assembly to identify their gifts and abilities so that they can do whatever they can to further the vision of the church. For the church to continually say they want the husband, but then say, either directly or indirectly, that the wife is not wanted at all is to invite trouble. This inevitably causes problems in the home, with a tug-of-war going on between church and marriage, and creates a no-win situation for everyone involved.

It may not result in much conflict if a minister's wife is only called to bake cookies (unless she hates to bake). But if there is any kind of specific call on her life that is unfulfilled, it will create an untenable situation if she has no chance to use her gifts and abilities in her local church. How would anyone feel if they were continually watching others being used while they sat on the sidelines, sometimes for years, without anyone encouraging them, or even acknowledging that they had any abilities that would be helpful?

I'm not maintaining that a wife should have the opportunity to do things just because her husband is a member of the board of deacons. But on the other hand, if a wife's gifts are neglected, there will be a source of good help that is overlooked, resulting in the church being diminished and a valuable resource becoming discouraged and unfulfilled.

This brings up another point that applies to everyone: what if someone has gifts and abilities in one or more areas, but those gifts and abilities are not presently needed? Are these people ignored altogether, or just kept on the bench in reserve, or perhaps directed to some other area where there is a need, but where they may not feel gifted or talented?

People who are genuinely interested in serving will do just about anything to move the vision forward, even if it means doing something that they may not feel equipped to do. However, the core of their calling, as exhibited by their gifts and abilities, cannot be denied or suppressed forever. Proverbs 18:16 says a man's gift makes room for him. If a gift is not recognized or appreciated in one place, it will be recognized someplace else.

If no opportunity to develop a God-given gift or fulfill a God-given desire is forthcoming where a person is, that will make it more likely that they will be tempted to move on to where another opportunity may be available. It takes a particular largeness of heart to subordinate a gift or calling to someone else. It takes a great measure of grace to do that for a long period of time, which may be why we see it happen so seldom in the body of Christ.

If believers are serious about being used by God for maximum impact, there will come a time where they must make a choice between using a heavenly gifting and allowing it to be extinguished through disuse. This creates a dilemma that may be impossible for them to resolve without help.

You may be currently serving a pastor, but you may feel that you or your spouse should serve in a different way. Perhaps you are completely unsatisfied and unfulfilled where you are currently serving. Talk to your pastor, or someone in leadership over you, before coming to any conclusions about what you need to do about it. You may be surprised how much helpful insight they can give you about what you are feeling or experiencing. Whatever you do, don't allow bitterness and resentment to creep into your relationship with your leadership. Keep the lines of communication open and let them know what you are thinking.

MONEY MATTERS

Here's another issue that often becomes a problem for support ministries: what if there's not enough money? There is more information available from a Christian perspective about money management than ever before, and it's not my intention to try to duplicate all that has already been written on the subject. I do have some suggestions that I believe will be helpful, and I've included them here because it's often up to a minister's wife to deal with the difficult and thankless task of trying to manage a household on a helper's wages or salary.

If you don't have a budget, by all means develop one. There is no better way to know where your money is coming from and where it's going. But you need to do more than just scrutinize and try to maximize the income side of the ledger. It's always easier to spend less than it is to make more. Look for ways to cut down your expenses. However little you are spending, you can always spend less. Matthew 7:7-8 says that those who seek, find. The other side of this is if you don't look, you will continue to be oblivious to the holes in your bag.

If you don't know how much you're spending in a certain area, such as groceries or gasoline, keep receipts and total them in each category on a monthly or quarterly basis throughout the year. This will give you a more accurate picture of how much it realistically costs to live, and where you can make adjustments. You might be surprised by how much those double latte almond mocha caramel cappuccino beverages really cost over the course of a few months.

Finances, or the lack thereof, can create a lot of conflict between a ministry helper and spouse, especially if one of them makes most of the money, and the other one pays most of the bills. A husband who is also the breadwinner may feel as though he is always a failure because he doesn't think he's making enough money to keep the household running. A wife who pays the bills may feel condemned because she can't stretch the income to cover all the expenses.

Husbands and wives need to talk to one another about these challenges in a way that doesn't leave them feeling accused or inadequate. They must come to some sort of agreement about how the finances are to be handled—or juggled, if necessary—to keep the bills paid. And they need to come into agreement in prayer and use their faith to rise above their circumstances. I have never known God to fail any couple who puts His kingdom first, asks Him for wisdom in financial decisions and trusts Him with their financial affairs.

At one time, my wife and I had squirrels in our attic because of holes in our home's soffits. At the same time, the hot water heater blew up, the transmission went out in our washing machine, and we were told the heating system in our home needed to be upgraded to keep from overloading our heat pump. While all this was going on, the more reliable of our two vehicles was sitting in our front yard, because we couldn't afford to get it repaired. We were also in the process of paying off orthodontic services for all three of our children, who were enrolled in a private school, with the tuition that went along with that commitment. A big night of entertainment for us back then was pizza (two large one-items for ten bucks) and a movie—at home on videotape, which we could rent three for a dollar.

From our perspective, we felt that we were actually making progress, because by that time, we had a second-hand bed that held together by itself. The one we had previously featured a footboard that needed to be tied with rope to keep it from falling apart.

I was working full-time and more, and Paula worked, as well, to pay for our children's tuition. It was a challenging season in our lives, and we didn't save a lot of money (in fact, we didn't save any), but we made it through. Looking back, I'm not sure how we made it, but God was gracious and faithful.

If you're young, healthy and don't have a lot of responsibilities, you may not feel the need for either health insurance or life insurance. But if you're married, purchasing a home or have children, you are well-advised to have both. There are considerable, and to many, unacceptable risks in not having insurance.

Regardless of how expensive insurance policies may seem, they aren't nearly as expensive as the financial exposure of being without them. I have talked to countless people over the years who have regretted not having the necessary amount of insurance to assist them in the event of a catastrophic accident or an unexpected death. Even a routine medical procedure or brief hospitalization can cause irreparable financial hardship without insurance coverage.

Working in the Lord's vineyard may not be the most lucrative occupation. Those in ministry derive their income from the tithes and offerings of those who give to God's work. Certainly, there are rewards that go beyond any paycheck, but the electric company won't take the good will of the church members as payment for a utility bill. As a support minister, you must maintain a good report in the community, which involves fulfilling your financial obligations promptly. You'll only be able to accomplish this through conscientious and vigilant oversight of your financial affairs. You can benefit from the strength of agreement when this is handled jointly, since you and your spouse, according to 1 Peter 3:7, are heirs together of the grace of life.

CHAPTER 4

Sheepdogs Gone Bad

The sheep farmers where I lived when I was young were upset. Economic pressure on family farms had been growing for years, and increasing incidents of sheep predation were causing additional financial strain. Some people blamed a burgeoning coyote population, but a growing body of evidence indicated that dogs were causing most of the problems.

When a group of farmers went to the courthouse to ask the county commissioners for their help, they encountered a small but determined band of animal rights activists. "We're concerned about the welfare of the dogs,"[3] their leader was quoted as saying. I couldn't help but wonder if it ever occurred to them to be concerned about the welfare of the sheep.

Subsequent investigations revealed that many of the sheep deaths were due to dogs—not homeless dogs turned out in the countryside, but dogs that lived on some of the very same farms where sheep were being mauled to death. What an unlikely scenario: old Shep by day—faithful farm dog and family pet, lounging under the front porch—and a vicious and bloodthirsty nemesis of every herd of sheep in the township by night. Sometimes it was hard to convince people that the dog that played so eagerly with all the children and barked an alarm at every visitor that came down the driveway was the same one that was killing the flock.

Once a dog developed a taste for sheep, from eating them, or more often just chasing and worrying them to death, it was virtually impossible to trust them again. Most farmers never tried, but resorted to the ultimate remedy for a sheep-killing dog, which was generally a vaccination—with lead.

Unfortunately, there are some men and women who have been in ministry, both in leadership and helping roles, who stop living to serve the sheep of God's pasture and begin to exploit them instead. This exploitation may happen in different degrees, but it is all ungodly and leads to destruction. When someone points out the damaging behavior, those who are under the offender's influence may object. They have grown to trust that person, and they will probably be suspicious of anyone who doubts that trust.

These offenders may be those who have been in the church for years, or they may be relative newcomers. In almost every case, it is a person who has been given credibility with the congregation by the pastor or other leader within the body of believers, which makes it that much more difficult to detect.

ANOINTED ASSISTANTS

Some scenarios with subordinates lead to division in a church more easily than others. One of these scenarios can develop when, as a church becomes established and grows, a pastor begins to look for help in fulfilling ministry tasks. As time goes on and the workload increases, he may look for another minister who is willing to help him. In many cases, this helper becomes known as an assistant pastor. However, this may not be what the pastor needs first.

It is unlikely that a pastor will need another preacher or pulpit minister until the church grows to a certain size. There is no hard and fast rule about this, but I would venture to say that this will be when attendance is in the hundreds, not in the dozens.

The most valuable person a pastor can have to help him, at least initially, is an anointed office assistant. Preachers are a dime a dozen compared to people who will give attention to detail and be diligent in making and maintaining accurate records. This person may not need to be in the office every day, especially when the church is small, but they must be someone who is conscientious about their work, since there are a thousand details to nail down in any growing ministry.

Kingdom work is serious business and needs serious attention, whether it is confirming funeral arrangements or keeping track of attendance in the nursery.

Sheepdogs Among the Flock

One of the greatest needs in the body of Christ is people who can make decisions and administrate a variety of responsibilities effectively. Not everyone who is called to ministry is called to preach. If you have an ability or even an inclination in the area of administration, I encourage you to develop it. You will be worth more than a half-dozen preachers in any church, and you will multiply the effectiveness of any pastor. If you doubt this, try this little test: ask your pastor who would be more valuable to him — someone who can only do the things he can do and enjoys doing, or someone who can do the things he can't or doesn't want to do?

Small groups are another scenario that needs to be closely monitored. They can be great training grounds for leaders and a wonderful means of evangelism and church growth. They can also be hotbeds of gossip, rebellion and division.

Group leaders should be selected only after much prayer and careful deliberation. But even if all your leaders are of impeccable character, problems may still arise in small groups due to others who are invited. Some of the invitees may be would-be pastors who also see a terrific opportunity for church growth: theirs, not yours. Trustworthy sheepdogs need to circulate among small groups frequently. If they are ever met with an unwelcome or even indifferent attitude, it is a caution sign that warrants additional scrutiny.

TROUBLE BREWING

How can you tell that trouble is brewing among those who are supposed to care for the sheep? The problem usually begins gradually, with little comments or innuendoes that seem innocent enough when they are made, often being passed off as being in jest. However, in time a pattern begins to emerge, but those who suspect something is amiss may be reluctant to speak up.

There are several reasons these indications that something is wrong may be overlooked or ignored. Nobody wants to be known as a nitpicker—because, after all, love thinks the best of everyone. Sometimes nobody points out inconsistencies because they feel like they have less credibility than the offender has. Sometimes it is because they have nobody they can trust to confirm that their ideas are valid before bringing the situation to the attention of the pastor or another leader.

Sometimes the ungodly one has been a close friend, comrade, colleague or even mentor, and any suggestion of untoward activity would be regarded as a breach of friendship or covenant. Sometimes any questions about the propriety of another's behavior would be seen as a betrayal of loyalty or trust and would result in sanctions against the person raising the questions, including dismissal, a ruined reputation or some other damaging consequence.

Regardless of who the person is or why they do it, death will always occur when sheepdogs start to prey on the sheep. This preying can take the form of money or favors being suggested, hinted at, asked for or demanded by the person in a position of authority. Sometimes expectations of intimacy enter into the relationship, regardless of the age, sex or marital status of either person involved. What is even worse, once a sheepdog develops a taste for sheep, it is difficult, and usually impossible, to break them of it. Why should they continue to serve and make sacrifices when the people who are trained to trust them give the things they want so willingly, even at the risk of their own well-being?

What can be done with a sheepdog who forsakes the care of the sheep, and instead begins to destroy them? Much has been said and written about the readiness of the body of Christ to destroy and devour their own wounded warriors, and of course we should attempt reconciliation whenever possible. Our fallen brothers and sisters in the Lord need repentance and restoration.

However, in any case, they should be kept away from any position of responsibility with the people until they have been given time and space to allow the fruit of repentance to be developed in their lives. They must also have the opportunity to go to those in authority over them and accept accountability for their behavior in order for restoration to take place. This takes a greatness of spirit and a willingness to forgive on the part of the leader who put them in a position of leadership in the first place. Trust has been destroyed, and time is needed for it to be restored.

The perspective of the shepherd needs to be considered as well. How should a pastor who bears the weight of responsibility for those God has entrusted to his care feel when one that he has discipled, taught, walked with, loved and elevated to a place of leadership betrays his trust and begins to devour the ones for whom the pastor has given his life? He has a mandate to remove the offending one and provide an opportunity for repentance to be walked out. That sounds good in theory, but it may not work out in practice.

Unfortunately, in real life, very often the offender becomes the offended and brings a railing accusation against the shepherd, either in public or in private discussions with the very people he has sworn to serve. This leads to nothing but dissension, division and death, and should never be named among the saints of God.

In a scenario such as this one, the pastor may have no choice but to require that the person find a place of repentance elsewhere. The safety of all the people God has placed under his care is more important than any individual, regardless of how talented they are or how faithfully they have served. Too often when this happens, the offender draws some of the people away with him who identify with him in his offense, and they become even further alienated and isolated.

In these instances, a shepherd has no choice but to immediately release the leader from their responsibilities in the local flock to prevent further devastation from occurring. If this seems hard, keep in mind this scriptural principle: to whom much is given, much shall be required. The greater responsibility rests upon the one in the position of authority, and the consequences of a breach of trust will be greater. There is no way a pastor can allow an assistant who has harmed the sheep and is unrepentant about doing so to stay in a position of authority.

Ultimately, it is the pastor himself who will have to give an account for his stewardship, including the behavior of the ones under his supervision. If sheep are being eaten during the shepherd's watch, he will be the one who will be required to give an account to God for it, regardless of who has been doing the eating.

Sometimes a different situation develops after the offending one has been removed from a position of responsibility for disciplinary reasons. There are times when the sentence, so to speak, is being served, but the offender is secretly building his agenda and networking with those he has met as a result of his position in his current opportunity to further his ministry elsewhere. In some cases, the "elsewhere" is in the same city or community. This is a particularly loathsome form of betrayal out of which no lasting good can come.

In any event, the opportunity for resignation or removal, if it is necessary, should be handled as quickly and quietly as possible. Repentance should be the goal, and if it is forthcoming, in many cases restoration can be an option in the future. However, sometimes the breach is so great it is unlikely the leader could ever have a credible ministry to that flock again, and the need to move on should be explained as carefully and redemptively as possible. At no time should voices be raised in anger, or recrimination sought. This is kingdom business, and it should be handled in a Christ-like and professional manner.

These kinds of problems also create conflict for those who have served alongside a leader who has gone astray. What will you do when a fellow sheepdog is found with mutton between his jaws? What should your attitude be when a colleague, sometimes for many years, falls into sin?

The principle that you must keep in mind in these cases is to follow the lead of the shepherd. You cannot be more loyal to the person in error, regardless of how long you have known him or how good a friend he has been, than you are to the leader of the flock. This may result in friendships being strained or severed.

When this happens, your primary consideration is this: what has God told you to do, and with whom? Stay with the word God gave you, regardless of how badly it hurts your flesh. Other people may come and go, but the call of God on your life is constant. The needs of the people you serve continue, and it is more important than ever that they see someone holding steady in the midst of turmoil, especially when the upheaval involves a leadership position in the church staff.

Sheepdogs Among the Flock

There are no absolute time limits to be adhered to in dealing with these issues. The things that need to be seen are a repentant heart and a changed attitude, especially in those who deal with the people of the church. This must be verified by the pastor, not only by outward appearance and performance, but in the attitudes and intentions that cannot be seen, but can only be known by a keen and discerning heart. Sometimes an offending brother or sister can be reconciled in a matter of a few months, but unfortunately, sometimes reconciliation can never be accomplished. There may be times when genuine repentance is not being acknowledged by those in leadership, but more often it is because it is not being fully walked out in the life of the one who has committed the offense.

WHY DO THESE THINGS HAPPEN?

What makes some people in leadership depart from caring for others and only care about themselves? Why do some people lose sight of the vision God originally gave them to serve and protect God's people? There are many reasons this happens, but three of the most significant reasons are pride, money and sex.

One of the first and foremost problems that cause a helper to forfeit his charge and begin to take advantage of the sheep is the matter of pride. This may begin with an ungodly comparison that a helper makes between his leader and himself. He sees what he thinks are the rewards of being behind the big desk and begins to ask why he doesn't or shouldn't have those same rewards himself. He then begins to use his position to make decisions or take actions that he feels will move him in that direction. These actions are not only unwarranted, but contrary to the well-being of the sheep. In doing so, he takes himself out from under the authority of those over him and begins to rebel in words and deeds.

If you want to be the one in charge, you will need to talk to your pastor about what you have in mind. He will surely have some ideas about it. There are organizations that specialize in church planting, but you will have to go through the process they require to start something new. In any case, if you plan to start a church after serving in a church, go somewhere far away (a few miles is not nearly far enough), where you will not disturb those whose trust you were given by your pastor, before you hang out your shingle and start having services. Don't stay close to the same church or community. To do so will inevitably cause conflict and tempt some who feel an affinity with you, or who just want to start some new venture, to separate from their church and join you.

Some people will follow you whether you ask them to or not. Don't try to hide behind the excuse that you didn't invite them. The fact that you are still in the area sends a message to them, and they may head off in a different direction than God has planned for them just because you are still around. Someone will answer to God for disturbing their peace. Don't let that person be you.

Sheepdogs Among the Flock

Another scenario can arise when the helper makes a comparison between what the pastor or other leader has and his own circumstances regarding money and material blessings. This will lead to all kinds of temptations, and money will always be at the center of them.

Home visits might become opportunities for personal appeals. Mailing lists or other information might be used for personal purposes. Generous donors might be solicited, and suggestions made to them about needs or desires that the poor helper has put off because of his sacrifices for the gospel's sake. Increases in pay might be requested or demanded. Probing questions about the salaries or economic status of other staff members might be asked.

If you are employed at the church, why would you chafe or complain about compensation to which you agreed before you took the job? If you're a volunteer, the very basis of the term means you fulfill your duties without expecting to be paid. In either case, money should not be an issue. If you need more money, ask God, not your employer. God is where your help comes from anyway.

Are there cases where a pastor or other leaders will not recognize the increasing value of a diligent helper and resolutely refuse to increase their wages or salary? I'm sure there are. But can you honestly demonstrate, in quantifiable terms, that you are more valuable to your employer than you were a year ago? In that case, you have a choice to make. If you think you can make more money somewhere else, and money is the thing that motivates you beyond all other considerations, you may need to move on.

Keep in mind that there may be external factors that keep a church or ministry from being able to increase anyone's salary—especially if economic distress is occurring in an area or even in a nation. When times are tough, charitable giving is usually the first thing most people eliminate when prioritizing their use of money.

The third area that causes problems is sex. More men and women are working together in the marketplace than ever before. This leads to situations that can cause both men and women untold grief—especially those involved in ministry.

As I have mentioned elsewhere, men and women who are not related should never be in certain situations that would compromise their reputation or cause their integrity to be questioned. Stringent safeguards are necessary in this area due to the pervasive influence of our morally loose culture.

Traveling in ministry can lead to compromising situations, especially when you are traveling alone, which is never ideal. A traveling companion is not only advisable, but at times invaluable. The accountability factor is far higher when someone else knows where you are and what you're doing. More than one preacher has fallen from lofty heights because they spent too much time in a motel room alone—and found a way not to be alone when they should have remained alone.

Sheepdogs Among the Flock

But you don't need to take a trip to stumble. More than a few in ministry have fallen prey to sexual temptation without ever leaving home.

Be careful of your choice of entertainment, wherever you are. Television used to be the main weapon the devil selected to overwhelm a minister with sexual temptation. Now it is the Internet, and temptation exists anywhere there is a laptop, tablet or cell phone. Don't let what should be helpful and useful technology become a portal to hell in your life.

Read the admonitions throughout the book of Proverbs to see the end of ungodly sexual behavior. And remember, no action ever took place without a thought behind it first.

It is worth whatever restrictions are necessary to see to it that you maintain your integrity and keep yourself free from fatal distractions. Your name does not have to appear on the list of sheepdogs gone bad.

CHAPTER 5

Trustworthy Sons
And Traitorous Sons

One of the most remarkable incidents in Abraham's life is recorded in Genesis chapter 18. Three men came to Abraham's tent and talked to him about God's plan to make a great nation of him. As the narrative continues, we realize that they were not men at all.

Abraham recognized the heavenly nature of his visitors and entreated them to stay while he prepared a meal for them. They began to explain to him how he would become a great nation: he and his wife Sarah would have a son even in their advanced age. In verse 19, the Bible says that the reason God could bless Abraham this way was because:

I chose him, and he will instruct his children and his household after him to keep the way of the LORD by doing righteousness and justice, so that the LORD may bring to Abraham what He promised him.

Sheepdogs Among the Flock

What we do as fathers and sons, both naturally and spiritually, is of utmost importance to the furtherance of God's kingdom. I have had the opportunity to observe many sons and daughters raised in preachers' households who feel a call to ministry. There are both challenges and benefits related to this situation.

THE CHALLENGES

One of the challenges is familiarity. Nobody knows parents better than children. You may be able to hide from people at work, at school and at church, but you can't hide from your own kids. They see you for who you really are—warts and all.

This familiarity can keep children from having the respect for their parents they really deserve. I don't believe that children need to call their fathers "Pastor" in the church, even though if they did I wouldn't say it was wrong. In any case, children should realize what a positive impact their father's life has had on many people in and out of the church. I regard it a high honor to be able to serve a man of God. How much more worthy of honor would he be if that man were not only my pastor, but also my father?

In most families, there is a natural inclination to favor a natural son. The son may not see it that way, especially if the father is determined to prove he is not showing favoritism by going out of his way to place greater expectations on the natural son than on anyone else.

Sometimes there are unresolved conflicts in ministry families. Before you recoil in shock and dismay, think about some of the unresolved conflicts in your own family. Preachers are people, and they have problems just like everyone else. As in other families, these problems can at times involve the relationship between parents and children. It can be difficult for children to realize that some of these problems are not unresolvable, nor are they unique to ministry families.

Another challenge is when children are involved in conflicts their parents have with others. They are sometimes aware of the details of these situations or overhear these issues being discussed. Children who see or experience these things can have difficulty separating the way they think things should be and the way they really are.

At other times, children raised in ministry homes are just not drawn toward ministry, and they don't sense a calling on their lives to be involved in ministry the way their parents are. Ministry is not hereditary. Just because you are a minister doesn't mean your son or daughter will become one. Your responsibility is to encourage them to follow the will of God for their own lives, whatever form that takes.

If God speaks to you about your children, as He often does, don't make that word an ultimatum. If you do, your children may spend more time running from God than they do following Him. They will feel handicapped if they are expected to follow your dream for their lives instead of their own. A father's season of life, responsibilities and opportunities are different from that of his children. He can be blessed by their successes and achievements, but they must be theirs and not his.

Here's another thing I have noticed: ministry children, especially sons, tend to feel a great deal of pressure to conform to other people's expectations of them. This seems to reach a crisis during the teen years, just when it is the most unwelcome and troublesome.

In response, some young people feel the only way they can cope is to develop their own persona, often one quite different from that of their parents. This desire to develop their own identity can be at the root of issues that arise between parents and children. Sometimes this is taken to such an extreme that the adolescent completely repudiates his parents' lifestyle and does things that are uncharacteristic of Christians just because they don't want to be thought of as being the same as their parents. As you can imagine, this causes no end of trouble for those in ministry, including sleepless nights, tears and agony in prayer.

I used to think that every failure on the part of the children could be traced back to their parents' failure to administer scriptural discipline or to provide consistent nurture, and I was dogmatic about it. Then I had children of my own who grew into their teen years. Suddenly I was reevaluating the claims I had made so confidently just a few years before.

Today, I realize that at a certain point in our children's lives they will have to make their own choices about how they are going to live. Those choices are made easier by the godly and consistent example of parents who exemplify love, compassion and forgiveness. But regardless of how good a job parents do, children can still choose to turn aside from the path they have been shown. I pray it doesn't happen to you, but if it does, that does not automatically disqualify you from ministry, and it doesn't indicate that you have done a bad job as a parent.

If you have a child that has gone astray, don't ever stop loving them, and don't ever stop believing that a gracious and forgiving God will show them the way home. Never give up on God, and never give up on your children. Don't leave them in the wilderness without your influence. I believe God will honor your faith, and your patience will be rewarded with a happy reunion, either here or hereafter.

THE BENEFITS

Don't think that it is impossible to raise children who will want to work with you, though. I have seen wonderful things happen when parents and children work together in ministry. Even though fathers and sons or mothers and daughters may see things differently and have different solutions for the same problems, there is something redemptive about parents and children working together to spread the gospel. In fact, some of the strongest churches I have seen are those who have family members working with one another in the ministry.

Sheepdogs Among the Flock

For one thing, start-up has usually been accomplished by the time children are old enough to become involved in the work of the ministry. The heavy lifting of beginning a work is in the past, and the younger ones can enjoy the fruits of their parents' labor. This can be a mixed blessing.

A caution here is to make sure the history of the ministry is known to the children. Otherwise, they may not know the price that was paid to produce what they see today—they were too young to remember. They may gain the impression that growing a ministry is effortless. Without an understanding of what it took to bring things to where they are now, they may make serious mistakes in judgment because they don't appreciate the opportunity they have been given. They have not had to make the same degree of sacrifices those who went before them had to make.

There are no better learning opportunities than when a young man or woman works under the guidance of an experienced minister who also loves them unconditionally and wants nothing more than their success.

I remember a story about H.L. Hunt, a businessman who a generation ago was worth $150 million. He owned a franchise in the American Football League, and put his son in charge. Not everyone thought that was a good idea. A friend telephoned H.L. Hunt and warned him that Lamar [Hunt's son] stood a good chance of losing a lot of money on the team.

"How much?" Hunt asked.

"About a million dollars a year," the friend said.

"Well, in that case," Hunt said, "it will take him 150 years to go broke."[4]

Another advantage to working with their parents is that sons and daughters will have ministry experiences readily available. They don't have to go anywhere or do anything out of the ordinary to gain experience—it's there waiting for them on a daily basis. This may not seem like an advantage, but it really is.

I know of a pastor who encouraged his son to work side-by-side with him every day in ministry, both on and off the platform. He wanted his son to eventually be able to lead the ministry. Unfortunately, the pastor became ill and passed away very suddenly. Even though he was terribly missed, the ministry did not lose ground, but in fact moved forward because the son was already prepared and ready to step into that role.

However, just because someone was raised in your household and shares your last name does not mean they will automatically assume the mantle of your ministry. Eli, the high priest in 1 Samuel, had two sons who were supposed to follow him into lifelong priestly ministry, but they were moral and ethical disasters. The prophet Samuel's sons weren't much better. Moses had two sons, but neither of them followed him into leadership in Israel. That honor was given to Joshua.

Sheepdogs Among the Flock

PROMOTION TO LEADERSHIP INVOLVES TRUST

A common lament of pastors is that they cannot find anyone, sons or not, who will take ownership of any aspect of ministry. Volunteers may not find the motivation to oversee an area where they serve, even though they serve conscientiously. Staff members may be misinformed about their prospects for promotion or may have miscalculated by assuming they were automatically next in line to supervise their area of service.

In order for a pastor to have the confidence he needs to allow someone to excel at any area in which they are involved, he must be able to trust them. What a relief it is for a pastor to know that when he gives direction, those directions will be followed. Happy indeed is the pastor who can do this with confidence.

Regardless of what kind of credentials a helper may have, there is no way a pastor can trust them with much until he has had a chance to see them interact with people and view their results. As with so many other things, this requires time to get to know people, and to have a track record upon which to base future decisions.

There are two errors that must be avoided here. First, it can be tempting to give responsibility to someone who has been loyal, just because they are standing in the court, so to speak. But if that person is not gifted in that area, or if they do not have an inclination to do what a leader asks of them, it may be disastrous to put them in charge.

Another error involves using someone who has just come into town and has a great reputation, but no record of accomplishment other than a resume or some recommendations. Someone once pointed out that although a recruit for a certain position had some drawbacks, they had a glowing resume. Another observer noted the reason the resume was glowing was because it was radioactive. The point here is that it is always a good idea to observe someone for a while before giving them more responsibility. It is easy to give it to them, but difficult to take it away if things don't work out as expected.

I believe we ought to promote from within whenever possible, since by doing so we have the opportunity to know those who labor among us, as 1 Thessalonians 5:12 says. This is not always possible, however, especially in areas where technical expertise is required, but it is desirable and a worthy goal toward which we can successfully work, especially if we invest in those around us.

One reason this doesn't happen is because pastors can become discouraged about sinking a lot of effort into helpers who bail out at some point in the process. It can certainly be frustrating for a pastor to see someone he invested in and helped raise up in his ministry become successful in a church in another community or state—or at a church across town, or even right across the street!

Sheepdogs Among the Flock

TRUST CAN BE BETRAYED

The issue of trust cannot be overemphasized. Pastors and those who help them must have trust as a cornerstone of their relationship. But this trust does not grow by accident. Pastors and their helpers must have time, spend time or make time to interact with one another. No time together means no interaction, no interaction means no knowledge, and no knowledge means no trust.

In 2 Samuel, we see that David did not really know his son Absalom and had no business allowing him to do what he did in Israel. His refusal to put a stop to it led to much bitterness and bloodshed that could have been avoided.

Absalom is an example of someone who was not only a son of the king, but also appeared to be the right choice as a successor. He was fair and well-favored, but as we know, outward appearance alone does not qualify someone for a position of responsibility. The third of David's sons, Absalom had the right look, the right bearing and the right countenance. From the outside, it looked like he could be and should be David's successor. He even had a remarkable feature that caused people to remember him—his long, luxuriant hair, which he only cut once a year.

Absalom became embroiled in controversy when Amnon, David's firstborn, raped Absalom's sister Tamar, then despised and rejected her. David was angry when he got the news, but apparently did nothing to bring justice to the situation. Absalom's heart became bitter that his half-brother Amnon could do such a thing to his full-blooded sister with impunity, and very likely began plotting Amnon's demise at that point. It took two years, but his plan finally manifested in Amnon's death. Absalom fled to his grandfather in Geshur for refuge. Even though David's heart was toward Absalom, he did nothing.

Three years later, Joab—David's army commander and Absalom's neighbor—enlisted the aid of a wise woman of Tekoa to illustrate to David his need to do something about Absalom's self-imposed exile. Absalom was brought back to Israel, but David refused to see him for two more years. When he finally did agree to see his son, who knows what passed between them? The king may have been aloof and indifferent at their meeting; Absalom may have felt like his father had betrayed him. Whatever happened when they finally met, Absalom's heart had apparently become fertile soil for the seeds of rebellion.

Seeing that his father was busy with the administration of his kingdom, Absalom worked his own methods unhindered. He undertook a calculated and comprehensive plan to steal the hearts of the men of Israel. The things he did to foment rebellion have been copied successfully by subordinates through the ages, causing untold grief for shepherds and their flocks everywhere.

Absalom hired chariots to go before him announcing his presence. This was not unusual for dignitaries in those days, but the substantial number of chariots Absalom employed indicated a great deal of self-importance and pride. Even though they did not all precede him at one time, it must have been an impressive spectacle for a lordly detachment of chariots to whirl down the road, loudly proclaiming that Absalom, the prince of Israel, was about to arrive. Coupled with his impeccable appearance and manners groomed in the king's court, all but the most discerning would have been awed and inspired by him.

Beware when someone looks like they have been polished too carefully. It could be that they have spent too much time looking at their reflection in the mirror. People come in all shapes and sizes. Just because they don't approximate someone's perception of what is ideal doesn't mean they are not the right person to do the job. I would rather be in the company of someone who was a little rumpled, yet had good character, than with someone who was always carefully put together on the outside, but was full of pride on the inside.

Following his ride through the city, Absalom would spend most of his time at the city gate. Before unsuspecting pilgrims had a chance to speak to the king about their business, he would intercept them, hear their story and flatter them with his attention and agreement. He would also tell them that the king was too busy to hear their case, but if he were judge, he would surely rule in their favor. No wonder many who encountered him gave him their allegiance. Not only was he a murderer and a conspirator, he was a master thief, stealing men's hearts away from his father right there under his nose in Jerusalem.

Trustworthy Sons and Traitorous Sons

Some of David's best and most trusted counselors were caught up in Absalom's rebellion. David was betrayed and abandoned by those who should have been supporting him through good times and bad. Instead, they turned against the king and committed themselves to an upstart usurper who was trying to take David's kingdom from him.

SOME TAKE UNDUE ADVANTAGE OF THEIR POSITION

Regardless of how fine a fellow Absalom seemed, he would have had no chance to have any influence at all in Israel if it had not been for his father. Everything he had and everything he was came not as a result of his own effort, but as a result of his family name. His credibility began with his father, not with himself.

We need to come to the same realization when we are working in another man's vineyard. There is no need for helpers to get some kind of attitude about themselves, thinking that the work could not go forward if not for them. A good dose of humility is essential for everyone who thinks they are indispensable. A proud look creates problems, not just for the proud, but for everyone who follows their example.

Absalom did what so many have become so adept at doing today—trumpeting their status as victims and exploiting people's sympathy for them instead of accepting personal responsibility for the way things are going in their lives.

Sheepdogs Among the Flock

Iniquity abounds, and bad things happen to good people. At times, the wrong ones are rewarded, and the right ones are overlooked. Welcome to life in a fallen world. Get over it, get up, go on and quit blaming everyone and everything else for wrongs that are real or imagined.

Absalom dispensed favor freely, but there was always a hook. He never gave anyone anything without recognizing the obligation under which it put them. Like a good poker player, he always knew the value of the cards he held. In time, he would call upon all those who owed him something, making them conspirators with him in his rebellion.

Despite his popularity, Absalom was a *divider*, not a *uniter*. He was the kind of person who could inflame passions, but not create a consensus. He was determined that what he wanted would be accomplished, not what was best for anyone else. His considered his agenda to be more important than his father's and more important than God's. He claimed as his own a kingdom that never belonged to him and took by force what others had worked years to build.

The difference between Absalom and David can be illustrated very simply. When David heard that Absalom was approaching Jerusalem, he left the city to keep it from becoming a battleground, which would have caused great havoc and the deaths of multitudes of innocent people — collateral damage, as it is known today. David chose to leave his capital rather than risk its destruction.

Absalom, on the other hand, did not challenge his father openly, but tried to overtake him by surprise at his dwelling place in the midst of Jerusalem. He appeared to be heedless to the devastation a battle in the city would cause. What would be the characteristics of a kingdom founded upon the principles of self-centeredness, betrayal and treachery?

Absalom made his plans and did his best to carry them out. Had it not been for divine intervention, he would have succeeded. Israel became embroiled in a bloody civil war because of Absalom's lust for power. His long hair, the symbol of his pride, at last led to his downfall. His hair became tangled in tree branches, causing him to hang helpless between heaven and earth. Despite the orders of the king, Joab killed him and ended the rebellion permanently.

Absalom could have been remembered as the fairest of David's sons, but instead his name has become synonymous with deception and division.

IT ALL STARTS SOMEWHERE

All those who would dare cause division in the house of God need to heed the lessons of Absalom's unfortunate career and untimely death. It is well-known that divisions in churches never begin without a beginner. Most of the time, this division begins with someone who is perceived as being in a position of leadership.

Numbers 16 chronicles the rebellion of Korah, Dathan and Abiram. They gathered 250 leaders of the children of Israel, and with this esteemed and respected body behind them, they took their complaint to Moses in the presence of the entire congregation. After Moses' response, they summoned all Israel to witness the next day. Then, the glory of the Lord appeared. This should have been a sign that the rebels heeded, but their hearts had already been hardened. They may have been misled enough to think that the appearance of God's glory was His stamp of approval on their rebellion. Perhaps they were convinced that God was going to judge Moses, and not them.

Suddenly the earth swallowed up Korah, Dathan, Abiram and all that belonged to them. In addition, fire consumed the 250 who stood with them in their rebellion against Moses. Those around them fled in terror from the judgment of God. The issue here is that rebellion did not start with the group—it started with the leaders before spreading to the congregation. Unfortunately, it has ever been so. No church split or splinter of which I have ever been aware started with someone sitting on the fourteenth pew. If someone like that leaves, they just leave. Sometimes their family members or a few close acquaintances may leave with them, but the disruption to the church as a whole is minimal.

On the other hand, if someone who is considered to be in a position of authority leaves, the influence they have is multiplied in direct proportion to the responsibility they have been given in the church. This has the greatest potential for disaster among a local body of believers. The error is compounded if the offended one who leaves goes across town or across the street and starts another work. If this happens, people in the church who identify with him might leave—even though God called them and set them in that body of believers. This should never be named among the saints of God, but it happens all too frequently.

The law of sowing and reaping is at work in these situations. When rebellion grows unchecked in a person's heart, it will spread and breed rebellion in others. Eventually, if there is no repentance, rebellion will be the hallmark of that life and legacy.

Korah, Dathan and Abiram died in an earthquake. Absalom died alone at the hands of those who used to be called his friends. In both cases, many others—who would have never been disturbed except for the rebellion of those perceived as leaders—died with them.

Someone will have to answer to God for the deaths of those who would have never had the thought to rebel except for some proud and insolent rabble-rouser who dared to thumb his nose at the authority God set in place. We would be better off if our tongue cleaved to the roof of our mouth rather than utter a word against God's work or God's leaders.

CHAPTER 6

Success in Succession

We hear a lot about the life and ministry of Moses, in both the Old and New Testaments. There is no doubt Moses was a remarkable individual, and his reputation in Israel's history was great. Moses stood at the forefront of millions of Israelites as their leader. God spoke to him as a man speaks to his friend. He was the great lawgiver—the human instrument through whom God gave His instructions to a nation—and to the world. It is little wonder Moses got more attention than anyone else during his lifetime. But Moses could not have accomplished nearly as much without the help of others, some of whom are never named.

On one occasion, seventy men went through the camp of Israel prophesying. We only know the names of two of them—Eldad and Medad. On another occasion, due to good advice from his father-in-law Jethro, Moses assigned leaders of thousands and leaders of hundreds to help administrate the affairs of the nation. These men remained nameless. But the most faithful and influential helper Moses had was a man named Joshua.

Sheepdogs Among the Flock

YOU MUST SERVE BEFORE YOU CAN LEAD

Even though Joshua is mentioned several times begin-ning in the book of Exodus, we first see him identified as Moses' minister in the book of Deuteronomy. Many people want to be known as ministers. Some will not do anything without a title (and then do very little after acquiring one). But we should always remember the word minister means servant. Some people put bumper stickers on their cars identifying themselves as a minister. I have never seen a bumper sticker that says *Servant*.

As a servant, if a task needed done, Joshua was the one who did it. Sometimes this meant standing in the place of the one he served as his delegated representative. At other times, it meant washing his master's hands or feet. Joshua did these things and more, and he did them for what most of us would consider to be an exceptionally long time.

You'll never be successful as a subordinate if you need to be noticed, or your name has to be mentioned, if you have to be recognized, or if you require special care and consid-eration.

Joshua went almost everywhere Moses went. When people saw them together, all the attention was inevitably focused on Moses. We never see any indication in the Bible that Joshua was troubled by this. He was secure in his role. He was not Moses, but he did have an important distinc-tion—he was next to Moses. When Moses was on top of Mount Sinai, Joshua was not with him. But Joshua did not remain behind with everyone else, either. He was somewhere on the mountain. And even though he was not the one on the top, talking to God, he was in a place nobody else had been in before.

Just because someone is not the head of an organization does not mean they are common. It takes a certain kind of greatness to stand with and support greatness in another.

Truly great leaders do not become great by surrounding themselves with sycophants or mediocre people. One of the remarkable things about Moses is that he recognized character in Joshua that needed to be developed and gave him opportunities to develop that character. The reason Moses sent Joshua to lead the fight against the Amalekites while he sat on top of the mountain was not because Joshua was expendable, but because he would need those leadership skills in the conquest of Canaan after Moses was gone. The prince had to win his spurs.

To be considered truly successful, you must raise up a successor. The failure of the church in this regard has contributed greatly to the crisis of leadership we have seen in the body of Christ. My generation, especially, is motivated by power above all else. We want to get it, consolidate it, and keep it—and we are not willing to share it with anyone else. This must change in order to perpetuate what God has begun on the earth.

Moses had every intention of leading the children of Israel into the Promised Land. He was disappointed when God's judgment kept him from crossing over Jordan. Part of what enabled him to accept God's sentence on his disobedience with such equanimity was the knowledge that there was someone ready to lead Israel into their inheritance.

TIMES OF TRANSITION IN LEADERSHIP

One of the most difficult seasons in the life of any local church is during a transition of leadership. I have seen more infighting, more bickering, more strife, more turmoil and more destruction and division during these crucial times than at any other. Ideally, someone should be ready to assume the leadership role in the church in the event a senior pastor can no longer serve. Unfortunately, this seldom occurs.

I have been asked many times to pray for or provide input to congregations who are without a pastor. One of the first questions I ask is if anyone in the congregation has enough experience and is respected enough to provide leadership, at least on an interim basis. Most of the time the answer is no, there is not. This may be because no one has been raised up, or because those who were being trained have left prematurely. It may be because those who were recognized as developing leaders took the opportunity to fracture the church instead of unifying it, and they took a group with them down the road to start another church.

Those who are being developed need to have a close relationship with the shepherd, but they should not be incapacitated if the shepherd is no longer there. After Moses' death, God spoke to Joshua and said, "Moses my servant is dead: get up!" Israel mourned Moses' passing for thirty days, but there came a time when they had to move on. Joshua's preparation made it possible for them to do so.

The most effective ministries are not those who always command the largest crowds. I believe the most influential ministers are those who raise up men and women and sons and daughters to carry the gospel message to places they themselves cannot go.

In Numbers 27:18-23, God instructed Moses to lay his hands on Joshua in the sight of all Israel. He also told Moses that some of the anointing on his life would be upon Joshua from that day forward. This is an important principle that we see in both the Old and New Testaments. Paul had Timothy, Peter had John Mark, Elijah had Elisha and Moses had Joshua.

It was important for this transfer to take place publicly, because Israel needed to see that Joshua was God's choice, and not just Moses' choice. There has been a great deal of speculation about how this kind of transfer is supposed to happen. Let me share with you several ways it does *not* happen.

An anointing can't be transferred just by the laying on of hands. There are many people who have hands laid on them by leaders, but don't get what Joshua got from Moses. I have seen far too many people wanting hands laid on them to get something for which they have no intention of making the necessary sacrifices to keep. As the old saints used to say, "You can have all of God you are willing to pay for."

Sheepdogs Among the Flock

If you have no job, no money and no prospects, it would be ridiculous for someone to buy you a home that would cost you hundreds of dollars every month in taxes. You would not be able to keep it if it were given to you. Even though such a gift might help you on a temporary basis, it would do nothing to resolve your long-term housing needs.

No leader can indiscriminately transfer the anointing of a well-developed ministry to someone else who is not in a position to walk in that anointing. They would never be able to carry it because the price is too high. They cannot afford it spiritually.

When I was in Bible school, I watched other students shove each other out of the way so a well-known minister could lay hands on them. Here's the problem with that: if you only have a six-ounce glass, six ounces is all it can hold, and there is no use trying to pour a gallon of water into it. The rest will just be wasted. In the same way, if your spiritual capacity is small, you will not be benefited by having great responsibilities and expectations thrust upon you before you are ready for them.

Jesus' disciples said they would be able to drink His cup and participate in His baptism. He assured them that they would, but not until they were prepared for it. We must wait on our ministry. The cake is not done until it has been subjected to the right amount of heat for the proper amount of time. God is the baker, and He knows the recipe. Too many have refused to stay in the oven of preparation long enough and come out half-baked.

If you want to receive from a great anointing, you should know certain things about yourself. First among these is knowing what God has called you to do, and who He has called you to become.

If you are called to be a shepherd, spend time around other shepherds. If you are supposed to be a Bible teacher, receive from those who have proven ability in that area. If you are called to evangelism, study the works and methods of successful evangelists.

You must determine the price you are willing to pay for the ministry you want to fulfill. Everything has its price, and it will always be greater than your initial estimate. In the case of ministry, it is not measured in dollars and cents, but in service and sacrifice. If what you want is to be a volunteer in the nursery, that is an honorable goal—and I have never seen a church that had too many faithful nursery workers. There is a certain price to pay for the anointing necessary to be successful in that area of ministry. But the price you will need to pay to be successful as the pastor of a church will be quite different.

There are no shortcuts or free passes on the road to successful ministry. Ministry done properly requires intense work and extensive effort. In any area of endeavor, you must be willing to learn things, forget things, hold on to things and relinquish things to be truly successful.

Being a ministry successor does not happen just because your mother or father was or is in ministry. It is an honor and a very humbling thing for parents to have children who want to follow them in ministry. But whether or not your children have a desire or inclination toward ministry, you can still raise up a successor. You may have a natural son or daughter who works in ministry with you, but that does not automatically mean they will become the shepherd after you. If you have a son or daughter after the flesh who is also a son or daughter in the spirit, you are most blessed. You can produce natural children, but you cannot produce spiritual offspring. That is the work of the Holy Spirit.

Some people have the idea that just because they have served for many years means that they will be in line for promotion when the pastor or other leader retires or moves on. This has been the cause of great disappointment for many people. Longevity does not automatically mean you will be the next pastor, music minister, nursery coordinator, chairman of the board of trustees or anything else.

I remember accompanying an evangelist to a church where he was holding a revival meeting. He asked to speak to the church's leadership before the meetings began. The pastor of the host church asked all his deacons to come to an informal gathering to meet the evangelist and hear from him about what he intended to accomplish during his time there. The pastor introduced all the men—most of them had been deacons for many years—and described them in glowing terms. When the evangelist asked them to turn to a Bible passage, half of them couldn't find the gospel of John in their Bibles.

Leadership is not something bestowed upon you just because you are there for a long time. While you are there, you should be learning, developing new skills and becoming more useful instead of just taking up space, filling a position or having a title.

People ask me all the time how I got to be the senior elder at my church. I tell them I just outlasted everyone else. I say that in jest, but some people think that is the only requirement for success and advancement.

So, then, how does proper and God-ordained succession in ministry happen? The question contains the answer: it must be God-ordained. The will of God must be acknowledged by both the leader and the follower. It is possible to attempt to explain this kind of arrangement in a written document, sometimes called a succession plan. It can be extremely helpful for a church to have written guidelines to follow in the event of a leadership vacancy. But even if such a document is available (and most of the time it is not) succession is something that must be understood between a leader and a successor.

LEARN EVERYTHING YOU CAN FROM YOUR LEADER

We can study the relationship between Moses and Joshua for principles that will help us in these kinds of circumstances. Unfortunately, it seems that the more or less seamless transition that occurred after Moses' death has been the exception rather than the rule. I believe we can do things to change this.

Sheepdogs Among the Flock

Joshua didn't help Moses for only a year or two, or even for a decade. He was by Moses' side for forty years, which must have seemed like a lifetime. Joshua was a patient man. Everything that Moses went through as Israel's leader, Joshua either participated in or observed firsthand. All of the incidents in Israel's journey to Canaan were life lessons for Joshua.

It never ceases to amaze and amuse me how little some people can learn from observation. It's as though they have their eyes open, but their minds closed to all but the most obvious lessons. Artisans at craft fairs the world over are in demand for demonstrating their techniques to those who have an interest in their occupation. Just having the chance to watch a master craftsman will result in valuable lessons for those who are willing to learn.

The same principle is true in ministry. Don't allow a day to pass without learning from those around you—especially from those over you in the Lord. Watch carefully. Ask questions about those things of which you are uncertain. Become the kind of person the Lord, and your pastor, is unwilling to do without.

Are there occasions where you will not be able to learn more from those who are directing you? Here's an example that may help answer that question.

One of my goals in high school was to play on my school's baseball team. My disappointment was unbounded when in my freshman year we didn't even have enough interested students to field a team. Then, during my sophomore year, our coach was someone who took the job by default and had neither the aptitude nor the inclination to be a baseball coach. It showed in our morale and our performance. We may have won two games all season—and that was more accidental than intentional.

When my junior year arrived, we had a coach who was dedicated, but not very knowledgeable. I endured a terrible hitting slump during the season and tried every way I knew to correct the problem. I was in the on-deck circle during one game when the coach said, "We really need you to get a hit."

"I've been having a lot of trouble lately and don't know what I'm doing wrong," I said.

I'll never forget his reply. "You're not hitting the ball," he said.

I didn't know much, but in that moment, I knew I wouldn't be getting any help from him. I explained what was happening to my older brother, who experienced success both as a high school player and a Little League coach, and he was the one who helped me resolve my batting problem.

There are times when those around you may not be able to give you the tools you need to succeed. They may have no experience or interest in the area you need to develop. That does not mean you are doomed to mediocrity or failure. There is always someone to whom you can turn for counsel and help.

Sheepdogs Among the Flock

It may be someone out of your regular sphere of inter-action. It may be a person whose advice you would not or-dinarily seek out or with whom you would not regularly choose to associate, but they may have the information you need. You might be surprised how open they would be to an honest inquiry from you about an area in which they have expertise.

Joshua had the opportunity to learn and receive from Moses' example. I have no doubt there were others who had input into Joshua's life, but none of them were as influential as Moses.

There was adversity aplenty on the way to the Promised Land—most of it the result of Israel's stubbornness, disobedience and outright rebellion. There were times when Moses' authority was challenged by those in the congregation who thought they knew it all. In every one of these situations, Joshua supported Moses and never expressed or even hinted at any kind of rebellious attitude. He followed his leader all the way to his appointed destination.

The turning point in Israel's trip to Canaan was after they arrived at Kadesh-Barnea. They had come straight from Mount Sinai and were at the border of the land God had promised to them. In fact, as far as God was concerned, it was already theirs.

Moses sent spies to go through the land and bring back a report about what it was like. The story is recorded in Numbers 13. The twelve spies all agreed on one thing—it was indeed a good land, flowing with milk and honey, just as God had promised. The majority report that caused the problem was what to do about the giants that inhabited the land. Ten of the spies said it was an impossible task, but two of them, Joshua and Caleb, had a different point of view. They urged the people to rise up and take their inheritance. But by this time, doubt and fear had crackled through the camp like flames of fire, and some people talked seriously of stoning the two men who were looking at their circumstance through the eyes of faith.

There will be times when supporting your leader is the least popular thing you can do. Joshua told the truth about his excursion into Canaan, but he was considered a threat to the well-being of the camp by the majority of Israelites. God Himself intervened and brought their intentions to a halt, but Joshua surely never forgot that the most people don't always make the best decisions. He was willing to sacrifice not only his popularity, but his life for what he knew in his heart was the right course of action.

Joshua had to endure the many years of wilderness wandering, even though he was not the cause of it. How many times was his soul vexed by the endless travel through the desert during that time? Yet he did it without complaint and stood by Moses through those dreary decades.

In time, the order came to quit circling and head north. Israel avoided confrontations with the Edomites, Moabites and Ammonites, but the kingdoms of Sihon and Og were a different matter altogether. It was time to fight, and Joshua was the field commander of the legions of Israel. They achieved significant victories before they ever crossed Jordan, and Joshua's reputation as a valiant warrior preceded him.

Joshua may not have felt particularly qualified as a man of war at the start, but by this time he was a seasoned veteran of every campaign Israel mounted during their journey. But his efforts were not to make a name for himself, even though that was a corollary of his success. He was fighting for all Israel, for his leader, Moses, and for his God. His victories were their victories. He was indeed a worthy successor to Moses.

This is an important lesson for all helpers. When we achieve success (not if, but when), it is not only for ourselves. We are contending for our leaders, for our faith and for our God. Let us never take the glory that belongs to others, but let us defer to those who are over us and give all the glory to Him who has called us to win in His name. If we do this, we will also be regarded as worthy, whether we move ahead as a leader, or continue as a helper.

CHAPTER 7

We Never Knew His Name

In Shakespeare's well-known tragedy *Romeo and Juliet*, two star-crossed lovers are denied the opportunity to develop their relationship due to their respective houses being at odds with one another. Juliet regrets this state of affairs and is soliloquizing about her fantasy of her lover giving up his name—as if all would be well if he would not identify with his family any longer. In what may be one of the most famous lines in the English language, she says "…that which we call a rose by any other name would smell as sweet."[5]

While it is true that a flower would be no less fragrant if known by some other name, that is not the case when it comes to people. We all understand that the essence of who you are as a person involves more than just your name. However, in most cultures, your name is the most common way that people identify you, and when a name is mentioned, people will automatically have some kind of impression about its bearer.

Sheepdogs Among the Flock

WHAT'S IN A NAME?

Proverbs 22:1 says: "*A good name is rather to be chosen than great riches....*" A name represents a person's reputation, so a good name means your reputation is good, and there won't be many opportunities that will be unavailable to you. On the other hand, a bad name means your reputation has suffered for some reason. It only takes one accusation, rumor or unkind comment to compromise a reputation that has been carefully built up over many years. If you don't have a good name, accomplishing anything of importance becomes much more difficult.

Even today, historical names have significance based on their reputation. Adolf Hitler's name evokes a negative response on the part of most people who know anything about him. Winston Churchill's name has the opposite effect.

Whether or not it seems equitable, your name is linked to your reputation, and it may have to do with things that happened before you were born. If your daddy and grand-daddy were scoundrels—with a penchant for drinking, brawling and conniving—you will have a tough time overcoming that reputation, regardless of how different your character is from that of the other men in your family. On the other hand, if you come from a line of morally upright, honest and hardworking men, people will tend to think of you that way whether you fit that type or not.

If you had siblings who went to the same school as you, chances are good that they predisposed your teachers to think about you in a certain way based on their behavior. If they were not good students, your teachers probably would have had a tough time thinking of you as a good student. On the other hand, if your siblings' performances were above average, your teachers very likely expected you to do well simply because you were from the same family.

Your name also represents your authority. When you open a bank account, the bank always requires you to put your name on a signature card. When you write a check, borrow money, purchase a certificate of deposit or do just about any other business with the bank, you have to sign your name. A check drawn on your account is no good unless it has your signature on it. A check made out to you cannot be cashed without your endorsement in the appropriate place on the back. Your signature or your name authorizes the financial institution to fulfill whatever transaction you require. Your name, for purposes of business, is you.

In ancient lore, men would not reveal their true identity to those they did not know or trust. They would use some other identifying term instead. According to legend, if someone knew your true name, that knowledge gave them power over you. Today, when people try to hide their identity, they conceal their true name.

I was once required to take a polygraph test as a job applicant. One of the first questions was, "Are you concealing any information about your true name?" I was surprised to think that anyone would do such a thing, but it happens more often than we realize. In fact, a burgeoning category of crime has arisen in recent years known as identity theft. Among other things, this involves assuming someone else's identity and making transactions in their name—that is, by the authority that their name represents.

If you've ever researched a name on the Internet, you have discovered that dozens, even hundreds of people can have identical names. Finding the person you are looking for—when so many others have the same name—can be an impossible task. Even names that seem to be unusual may be shared by many people. If your name is more common than most, you may find there are thousands of other people with your name.

One year we had two young ladies in the college where I was a faculty member who had the same first and last names. We thought it would be a simple matter to distinguish them by their middle names. The problem was that they each had the same middle name as well, so we had to be creative in discovering ways to make sure we made a distinction between them. This may not have been significant when it was an isolated incident in a classroom, but it would have been a real problem if their identities were confused when grades were being recorded.

If you have children, you probably spent a lot of time thinking about what you were going to name them. Perhaps you got a baby name book and looked at what all the names meant. Maybe you named your children after a family member or a hero of yours—someone whose character you admired.

In ancient cultures, people gave their children names that often described who the parents hoped they would become, or sometimes who they actually would become. The name Jacob meant heel-catcher, supplanter or defrauder. Born holding his twin brother's heel and eventually taking his brother's birthright, Jacob's name really did represent his character.

In medieval times, people were named after their occupation or location. Many of today's most common last names come from well-known or familiar occupations of ages past, such as a smith or a miller.

One of the benefits bestowed on believers in heaven is a new name—one that will be different from every other one among the multitudes who will be there. That name will no doubt reflect the particular characteristics you possess and the uniqueness by which you will be known. If you don't like your name here, and don't want to go through the legal technicalities of changing it, don't worry—God has a new name already picked out for you. In fact, there have been times when God changed people's names here on earth— just look at what happened to Abraham, Jacob and Peter. I think you will like the one He gives you.

Another blessing is that God won't have to search through some heavenly database to find you—He knows exactly who you are, and He won't have any difficulty distinguishing you from all His other children.

Sheepdogs Among the Flock

THE MAN WITH NO NAME

There are times when people don't have a name—or at least, we don't know what it is. A well-known celebrity cemented his reputation as a movie icon by appearing in several films known only as "the man with no name."[6] But just because a person's name is not known doesn't mean they aren't important. More than one character in the Bible had no recorded name, but that didn't keep them from playing important roles.

We see one such unnamed person in 1 Samuel 14:6-14. He accompanied Jonathan as his armorbearer. Even though his name is not known to us, he provides a fascinating example of a faithful helper.

In the days when kings passed their thrones on through inheritance, the son of the king, especially the firstborn son, was of inestimable value to the kingdom. Anyone who had the responsibility of helping and protecting the heir to the throne was carefully selected, and had to exhibit extraordinary courage, loyalty and vigilance. These servants had the responsibility of protecting the king's lineage, and the future of the kingdom was entrusted to their care.

But regardless of how sterling their characters, the armorbearers, as these men were known, were elevated simply because they were with the king's son. Their responsibility raised them to a position of greater prominence than they could have ever attained in any other endeavor. In old western movies, the faithful sidekick could always be found nearest the leading man in many scenes. In the same way, those who were entrusted as armorbearers were always found with the person they were helping. Their status was inevitably linked to the person they served.

What this means is you can gain an additional measure of credibility (or notoriety) by virtue of whom you serve. With every passing year, I am more aware that it's not what I know, but who I know and what they know that makes a difference in many situations.

A young man was having a great deal of difficulty trying to become established as a trader on the New York Stock Exchange. It seemed that nobody wanted to deal with a neophyte, and the other traders wouldn't even look his direction. In frustration, he sought the advice of an elderly gentleman who had made his fortune in the stock market and was known and respected by everyone who conducted business there.

The old man didn't grant him a private meeting, but instead asked him to accompany him on the trading floor in the middle of a busy day. They walked back and forth as the old man listened to the young man's concerns. After thirty minutes, the older gentleman placed his hand on the young man's shoulder and said, "Son, I don't think you'll have any more trouble."

The young man was frantic. "But you haven't told me how to gain the credibility I need," he said.

"Young man," the old trader said, "everyone in this building has been watching me talk to you for the last half hour. They'll deal with you now."

Sheepdogs Among the Flock

Your choice of companions can move you forward or hold you back. Old preachers used to share this maxim: "Show me who you run with, and I'll tell you who you are." 1 Corinthians 15:33 says, *"Do not be deceived: 'Bad company corrupts good morals.'"* The second half of Proverbs 13:20 says, *"...a companion of fools will be destroyed."* Ben Franklin said, "If you lie down with dogs, you will get up with fleas."[7]

On the other hand, if you spend your time in the company of the wise, some of their wisdom is likely to become yours. The first part of Proverbs 13:20 says: *"He who walks with wise men will be wise...."* Be careful with whom you associate. Seek out those who know more than you and are willing to share what they know. Life changing wisdom can be available to you by doing nothing more complicated than asking a respectful question.

Despite his bravery and his close association with Jonathan, the armorbearer had a great disadvantage—he had no weapon of his own. This was not a failure on his part, but a commentary on the deplorable state of affairs in his nation. The children of Israel had allowed themselves to be disarmed, while their enemies were well-armed. This has always been a recipe for enslavement. Beware of anyone who maintains that you must not be allowed the means to defend yourself and those who are dear to you. In this case, it took divine intervention to enable Israel to fight back against its enemies.

The armorbearer was obviously not depending on his ability with a sword to win a victory—his trust was in something else altogether. But when he finally got into the fight, he grabbed the first weapon he could get his hands on and pitched into the Philistines with great gusto. He was willing to follow his leader even though it looked like he was unprepared. Valor may take many unusual forms, and character cannot always be quantified in terms of numbers or physical stature. As someone said, "It's not the size of the dog in the fight, it's the size of the fight in the dog."

The armorbearer also had confidence in his leader. This is an intangible factor that is worth more than a multitude in any conflict. In an evenly matched contest, victory will most often go to those who have confidence they will win. The confidence factor can even help an individual or team overcome great disadvantages, and the lack of it can create real problems for those who look like favorites.

I remember a pastor friend telling me about his first boxing match. He hadn't been training very long before his handlers signed him up for a bout. They were counting on his height and reach advantage to make a decisive difference. His opponent did not share their point of view. When it was over, they had to tell him he was the winner, because he was too punch-drunk to recognize it himself. Even though he was victorious, it didn't do much for his confidence, and that was the last match he ever won. A few more beatings convinced him to take up tennis instead.

Sheepdogs Among the Flock

AN ARMORBEARER MAKES VICTORY POSSIBLE

Jonathan's armorbearer didn't consider the circumstances—he respected his leader's judgment, and even though the challenge looked formidable, even insurmountable, he refused to let his leader go into battle alone. Nor did he follow afar off, watching to see the outcome before committing himself—he was right there with Jonathan when the first Philistine came into view. He was not a fair-weather follower who only jumped on the bandwagon after success was assured. He didn't just celebrate the victory after observing the fight from a safe distance—he was on the front lines making victory possible.

Not only were the armorbearer's actions important, his words were also essential. When Jonathan explained to him what he planned to do, the man didn't raise all kinds of objections to what must have seemed like a risky and even ridiculous plan of action. He didn't come up with a score of reasons why it shouldn't be done. Instead, he told Jonathan to do what God had placed in his heart, and that he would be with him wherever his leader wanted to go.

This is an important lesson for all helpers. Great leaders are visionaries—they can see what others can't, and they aim for targets that others can't perceive. When they do, they don't need to be told all the reasons why a thing can't be done or shouldn't be done—they need those around them who will assist them in achieving their goals.

I'm not advocating that all the helpers become "yes men" who never do anything other than stroke the leader's ego, but nothing great can be achieved without someone imagining it and then making it happen. As helpers, we need to encourage our leaders, not become anchors around their necks. When everyone is in the same boat, all hands need to row in the same direction—and everyone needs to work toward the same goal, not sit passively by, or even worse, criticize the ones who are rowing.

The armorbearer was willing to follow his leader in a difficult and dangerous venture. The outcome was anything but assured. In fact, the odds were heavily against them. It is doubtful Jonathan could have achieved success without the armorbearer's help. He might not have even attempted it without someone to stand with him in his hour of need.

Two are better than one, for lots of reasons. The power of agreement is well documented in the Bible. When you face your adversary alone, there are many things that can go wrong, but when you have someone standing with you, it doesn't just add to your effectiveness, it multiplies it. Jonathan and his armorbearer not only won a victory for themselves that day, they created momentum that led to their enemies' defeat on a much larger scale. Who can tell what benefits may accrue as a result of your agreement with your leader?

As you know, the armorbearer's name is not mentioned, neither in this narrative nor anywhere else in the Bible. I'm certain he had a name, and Jonathan no doubt knew it, but it wasn't recorded. But even though we don't know what this faithful man's name was, we still know of his exploits from the record of no less an authority than the Word of God. The armorbearer wasn't concerned about whether anyone would know his name. He wanted his leader to experience victory, and he had an indispensable part in making that happen. We don't know who he was here on earth, but I am convinced we'll know who he is when we pass over to the other side.

We don't know if this armorbearer was with Jonathan when he finally fell in battle on Mount Gilboa. It is possible he could have been promoted or moved into a different set of responsibilities before Jonathan's life ended. Sometimes people will be assigned to help a leader for one project, one season or to help achieve one goal, then move on to another place or situation in obedience to God. This should never be a cause for frustration for either a shepherd or a sheepdog. Some people will come and go because they are on a temporary assignment at the direction of God.

I once knew a man who had been involved in dozens of jobs by the time he was thirty years old. I asked him about it, and he said that he would take jobs knowing they weren't going to last very long, because God put him there to witness to someone or encourage someone while he was working there.

I recall a man who helped us with a building project underway at our church. Even though he had been hired to fulfill a different role, he became essential to the oversight and management of a monumental task that was filled with unexpected problems. He worked day and night to see the project brought to fruition, and shortly after it was over, he moved on to what turned out to be even greater achievements elsewhere.

Jonathan's armorbearer passed into history as a little-known but essential part of God's plan for the nation of Israel. Your name may never be up in lights or engraved in stone, but as a faithful helper, you, too, have an important part to play in God's plan for the body of Christ. You may not experience fame or recognition on earth, but always remember that the heavenly record is not the same as the earthly record. Your name is surely recorded there, and your reward is reserved for you.

CHAPTER 8

Agreeing—But Not Alike

Other than Moses, Elijah was one of the two most revered people in ancient Judaism. This isn't hard to understand when you consider his résumé. He declared a drought, called fire down from heaven, defied wicked king Ahab and was taken to heaven by a fiery chariot. He had quite a career, and if many end-time preachers are correct, his ministry is not over yet. He achieved a lot of notoriety during his lifetime and is still referred to frequently.

Can you imagine what it must have been like being his helper? Who would give up a comfortable life to become what many would consider to be a flunky for someone famous? What kind of person would it take to stand beside a man like that?

It would take a farm boy named Elisha, the son of Shaphat. He was willing to walk with Elijah, because he must have realized that if you are called to be a prophet, one of the best ways to learn what you need to know is to be around a prophet. He couldn't stay on the farm and fulfill the future to which God had ordained him.

Sheepdogs Among the Flock

CUTTING TIES AND STEPPING INTO YOUR FUTURE

A mistake I have seen many young ministers make is that they continue to keep company with those who do not understand the call of God that is upon their lives. Not everyone is going to be able to go where you have to go. The sooner you learn this, the fewer delays you will have on your road. Walking with God will require some things of you—especially in terms of relationships with those who will hold you back from fulfilling your purpose.

A movie about a young pop singer from a generation ago involved a choice he had to make. He could either stay with his friends he had known throughout school, whose talents were mediocre and would only limit him, or he could say goodbye to them and rise to stardom because of his superior talent and ambition. It was painful, and his friends felt betrayed, but shortly after he cut them loose he made his mark on the music scene. They could not follow him where he wanted to go.

Elisha could have stayed at home and had a good life. He may have become the best farmer in all Israel, if God had called him to be a farmer. He would have had the respect and good will of his friends and neighbors. His parents probably placed their hope for the future in him and were very likely disappointed by their son forsaking the family farm and taking off after an itinerant prophet who always seemed to be in trouble with the authorities. None of these things kept Elisha from fulfilling the summons he received to help a man of God.

There are alternatives available to everyone. As free moral agents, we make choices every day that affect our lives and the lives of those around us. God won't force us to do His will—we can be born again, fulfill our own plans for most of our lives and probably still go to heaven. We just won't have any reward waiting on us when we get there.

Many who have been genuinely called by God have been turned aside by a romantic relationship, the lure of a good paying job, the promise of a college education, a house, a car or some other kind of material possession. How great the loss to the body of Christ and to the world when a ministry gift is stillborn because of selfishness.

Before he acknowledged the call of God on his life, Elisha lived a relatively simple life with a routine that was determined by the sun and the seasons. After he began to follow Elijah, he discovered that there was a lot of flexibility required in serving God as he was required to do.

I would never advocate that we add to or subtract from Scripture, but I have always maintained that there is a beatitude that someone forgot to record during the Sermon on the Mount.

It is this: "Blessed are the flexible, for they shall be flexed." Staunch and stiff-necked people will have an especially tough time staying happy about church work, since it will require a lot of flexibility.

Elijah always had people seeking him out and trying to have an audience with him. Kings sought (or dreaded) his counsel. He was in constant demand and had to organize his time to do everything God commanded him. He had to remain sensitive to the Spirit of God and be ready to move at a moment's notice. It was imperative that he obey God immediately and implicitly to obtain the required results.

This must have been difficult for a farm boy from rural Israel like Elisha. To have gone from the eldest son and heir on the family farm to a servant who was required to do the most menial tasks had to have been quite a change for him. He went from one lifestyle and set of responsibilities to another one in just one day. The learning curve was undoubtedly steep. Elisha must have handled the change well, since he persevered and didn't fall by the wayside.

One of my acquaintances in Bible college was a man from another Midwestern state. He took one look at the campus and was ready to go home. He said it was too ornate for him. He later changed his mind and stayed, but he wasn't comfortable around new things that looked nice. It was too much of a change from the things to which he was accustomed, and it hindered him from receiving all that God had for him.

God will surely ask you to do some things that make you uncomfortable as you follow Him. He may ask you to do some of them for a long time. Don't be troubled by that, but do all that is asked of you to the best of your ability. Your faithfulness, not your comfort level, is what brings a reward.

My wife and I don't play cards often, but when we do, we seldom partner with one another, since our approach to playing is quite different. I tend to be conservative, because I don't like to make mistakes that result in suffering loss. On the other hand, my wife takes risks that are downright scary. She wins most of the time.

I don't mean to reduce life and ministry to the level of a card game, but in this case, as in cards, so in life. There is a certain amount of risk involved in every kind of endeavor, and ministry is no exception. As the old saying goes, fortune favors the bold. Financial advisors will tell you the rewards you can expect are commensurate with the risks you are willing to take when investing your money.

Elisha took a significant risk when he left his plow and followed Elijah. He traded a life of relative certainty for a life of absolute uncertainty, but the rewards that resulted were beyond anything he would have known if he had stayed on the farm.

Let me be clear—I have no criticism of farmers. If God has called you to be a farmer, be the best one you can be, and do it for the glory of God. All of us will be rewarded based on our obedience in fulfilling God's purpose for our lives.

Sooner or later, though, you will be called upon to make the same kind of choice Elisha had to make. Will you hold on to what is familiar, or step out into a God-appointed, but daunting assignment?

Sheepdogs Among the Flock

SERVING IN OBSCURITY

As a ministry helper, you will have to deal with the misunderstanding and even criticism of friends and family members. They will want to know why you can't come to the family get-together on Sunday afternoon. They will ask why you work such long hours for what seems to be so little reward. They will compare your achievements, which may be obscure, to someone in your family who has his own parking space in the company lot by this time in life.

Don't allow yourself to be moved by any of this. Success can never be measured by comparing your life to someone else's. Your success depends on how well you fulfill the vision God places in your heart.

God instructed Elijah to find his successor and pointed out Elisha by name. Elijah lost no time in going to where the young man was plowing in the field with the last of twelve yoked pairs of oxen. Having this many oxen indicated Elisha's family was wealthy—it meant they had a considerable amount of land to plow. It would have required quite a lot of food to sustain two dozen oxen on one farm.

No doubt Elisha had at least a share of the family farm to look forward to as an inheritance. It might have been a grievous thing to walk away from such a life, but we see no indication that Elisha had any regrets. He might have had the opportunity to have regrets later, after he found out what kind of life he would be living and what he would be doing.

Agreeing—But Not Alike

As long as Elijah was alive, Elisha was bound to live in relative obscurity. A prophet's helper in those days was mostly a servant, serving rather than being served. There was something about the anointing of God on the life of Elijah that Elisha wanted, though, so he served with faithfulness and humility.

There are definite advantages to being in obscurity. When you are in the shadows, people cannot see you as easily. You are not the one in the spotlight, so you attract a lot less opposition. The adversary's flaming missiles are hurled at the leader, not at you. Being in the background also enables you to go about your business uninterrupted, doing what you are supposed to do without being distracted and drawing a lot of enemy attention.

Being in the shadows also means you are close to the one you are serving, which is where you can be most effective. Don't worry about not being in the light. People don't need to see you anyway—they need to see Jesus. If and when the time comes for you to step into the light, God will make you ready for that. Until that time, be content to stay in the back.

We don't know exactly what Elisha had to do while he was serving Elijah, but we know that on one occasion he was identified as someone who poured water on the prophet's hands. This indicates that he spent a lot of time doing menial tasks, instead of prophesying and preaching.

Sheepdogs Among the Flock

Here we learn a valuable lesson—much of ministry is not seen and rewarded openly. In fact, much of what is necessary in ministry is not recorded anywhere except in heaven. Ministry is not primarily what happens behind a pulpit.

A young man who graduated from Bible college returned home to begin youth ministry in the church where he grew up. He saw me some months afterward, held up his thumb and forefinger about an inch apart and said, "Elder Canfield! Tell these students that preaching is only about *that much* of ministry!"

Success in ministry begins with what happens in the private places—where nobody sees, and nobody knows except you and God. You can be successful in ministry without a pulpit, but you can never be successful in ministry without an altar.

I am certain that the idea many ministers have about ministry is backward. We want God to anoint our public proclamation and may become involved in strife and debate in order to get what we think is our fair share of pulpit time or platform opportunities. We revel in the compliments we get from those who think we have done a good job. If we are not watchful, we may emphasize this aspect of ministry to the neglect of other things that also provide necessary ministry to those we are serving.

We spend hours in prayer asking for a revelation to preach to the masses. We seek God for wisdom and understanding to proclaim His word with power. We ought to—

after all, preaching is vitally important. But is ministry to the sick or comforting those who are grieving any less important? Shouldn't we seek to do these things, and the thousand other things that ministry involves, with excellence? Ministry at its best is never about us, but always about someone else.

I was watching the movie *Gone with the Wind* with my family, and something struck me in one scene involving the doctor and his wife. The interaction between them was such a great bit of acting that I had to stop the tape (we had videotapes in those days) and point it out to my kids.

"Let me explain something to you," I said. "The difference between a good movie and a great movie is not how the lead characters play their roles. They are the ones making the big bucks, and everyone expects them to do a good job. The difference between a good movie and a great movie is how the supporting cast members do their jobs. They are not the ones who get the notoriety—sometimes they only have one small scene. But when they play their roles with excellence, then you have a great movie."

I believe the same thing is true for great churches. I don't believe you can have a great church without a great pastor. I do believe, however, there are great pastors who do not have great churches because the people around them are not doing their parts with greatness. When the people in the smaller scenes do what they are supposed to do with the same kind of attention to detail that the pastor does, then you will find a great church.

Sheepdogs Among the Flock

WALKING INTO THE DOUBLE PORTION

Elisha went from operating farm implements to operating in the anointing of God. This was quite a shift and required him to learn new things and acquire new skills. He probably did a lot of things wrong at first, and I can't imagine Elijah being a very patient instructor. But Elisha stuck it out and was rewarded for his service. Galatians 6:9 says, *"…in due season we shall reap, if we do not give up."* Elisha did not give up, and he was rewarded with a double portion of the anointing that Elijah had.

This does not necessarily mean you will be twice as anointed as your pastor, but it does mean you should perform your duties with excellence and humility. God has a reward in store for you as well.

Elijah and Elisha were as different as it is possible for two people to be, at least as far as their personalities were concerned. Elijah was a classic example of a maverick, a loner, an individualist. He insisted on doing things himself, probably to make sure they were done exactly the way he wanted them done.

Consider the challenge with the prophets of Baal in 1 Kings 18. Elijah rebuilt the altar, prepared the sacrifice, laid the wood in order and prayed the prayer that called fire down from heaven. He would have probably poured the water on the altar if he could have lifted the barrels by himself.

Elisha, on the other hand, was more of an administrator than Elijah ever was. He was always commissioning other people to act on his behalf—sometimes even letting them take his place in speaking a word or ministering to someone in need. When Naaman the Syrian came to see him, Elisha didn't even come out of his house, but sent his servant in his place. That's what made Naaman so angry. He thought he was important enough that the prophet would have seen him personally. It was only the good sense of his servants and the grace of God that allowed him to receive a miracle of healing despite his temper.

God can use everyone, regardless of what kind of personality they possess. God made you with certain characteristics, and He wants to use them for His glory. In fact, God will deliberately and strategically connect you with people who are not like you, so you can multiply your effectiveness for the kingdom of God.

I'll never forget the first time I took a personality inventory. For years, I wondered what kind of person I really was, and why. I desperately wanted to be different, since I was convinced I wasn't of much use to God. It was a revelation to me to discover the characteristics I displayed most often were consistent with my personality type. I now realize that those very characteristics I questioned so much enable me to interact best and be an effective complement to someone with a leader personality type.

Even though the results of the survey did not surprise me, it was a compelling thing to know that I really am acceptable to God. I don't have to strive to be like someone else to fulfill my purpose of being a ministry helper.

Sheepdogs Among the Flock

Elijah may have had a far more forceful personality, but Elisha did twice as many miracles as Elijah did. Both of them were genuinely called and anointed of God, but Elisha truly did get the double portion of anointing for which he asked. He may have also influenced more people during his life and ministry than Elijah did. Both were essential to God's purposes being fulfilled in their day.

CHAPTER 9

Single Mantle, Double Anointing

One of the most unconventional journeys in the Bible is recorded in 2 Kings 2. The time had come for Elijah to pass over Jordan and enter into his heavenly reward. It was time to pass the mantle of anointing to his faithful servant Elisha, a prophet in his own right. Even as Elijah and Elisha undertook this journey, passersby who met them on the road that day would have noticed nothing out of the ordinary about them. But before the day's end, one of them would be lifted from the earth by a heavenly conveyance, and the path of the one left behind would be almost as remarkable.

GILGAL

We're not told where Elijah and Elisha began their walk together that day, but we do know that Elijah's first destination was Gilgal. If they were traveling to the historical Gilgal where the children of Israel first stopped after their miraculous crossing of the Jordan River, it would have been located somewhere east of Jericho. Though some say there may have been another Gilgal, there is no record in the Bible of any other place with that name.

In any case, Elijah said God told him to go to Gilgal. Elijah told Elisha to stay behind. Elisha would not—and with good reason. They both knew that the day of Elijah's departure had come, and Elisha wasn't going to miss anything that was going to happen. There was something that he wanted that he had not yet received.

It is a well-known principle in life, as well as in ministry, that a lot of people start, but few finish. There are many who begin this race, but beginning is not the significant thing. No prizes are awarded at the starting line. It is only when we finish that we receive recognition. Elisha didn't just want to start—he wanted to finish. And to do so, he needed to move on from where he was.

Gilgal was significant, since it was the place where Israel received the rite of circumcision after their entrance into the Promised Land. It was impossible for this task to be completed during their wilderness wanderings, since they never knew when they would be required to move out during their journeys. In addition, they always had to be watchful for enemies who would have undoubtedly tried to victimize them had they been caught recovering from being circumcised while in the desert. It seems that God gave them a special grace to dispense with this expression of covenant keeping during the forty years in the wilderness. But once they arrived in the Promised Land, it was time for their commitment to be complete by means of circumcision.

Gilgal—which means *rolling*—was the place where the reproach of Egypt was rolled away from them. It was also the place where Joshua took his army after each campaign in Canaan. It seems it was a sort of temporary headquarters for him during his conquest of the land.

For the believer, Gilgal represents the salvation experience. It marks the spot where our sins were washed away, and we were made right with God.

Don't allow your pilgrimage to come to an end where you received right standing with God. There is much more to your life and ministry than just knowing your sins have been forgiven and you are going to heaven when you die. Go after all God has and pursue it with all your heart. Don't stop at Gilgal.

BETHEL

Elijah's next destination was Bethel. He told Elisha to remain at Gilgal while he went on at the direction of God, but Elisha came with him anyway.

Bethel was the city north of Jerusalem where God revealed Himself to Jacob after he had deceived his father Isaac into giving him the blessing that should have been reserved for his brother Esau, the firstborn son.

Bethel became known as the house of God. It is fascinating to me that in the narrative of God's visitation to Jacob, He showed him angels ascending and descending on a set of stairs between heaven and earth. From this, we know that angels are personally present on the earth. They were here then, and they are here right now. They have regular interaction between the earthly and heavenly realm—and they aren't limited to using stairs, either.

Bethel was a place of divine revelation and visitation. You would think that if Elisha were going to be tempted to stay anywhere, it would have been there—but he went on with Elijah.

We, too, need to move beyond our first revelation from God about our lives, our ministry, our relationships, our business, our family or whatever else God shows us. Many people are so exhilarated about hearing from God regarding a specific area of their lives that they stop moving and stay there. Elisha didn't, and we shouldn't, either. Don't stop at Bethel.

JERICHO

The next waypoint on their trip was Jericho. Jericho, of course, was that great walled city of antiquity that confronted the incoming Israelites when they crossed into the Promised Land. Tall and imposing, it was a formidable obstacle to anyone attempting to cross into the hill country from the river valley. It was a testament to the skill and cunning of men, but it fell by the power of God. It has forever after been recognized as a place of conquest.

Not only that, Jericho was also known as the City of Palms. It was a pleasant oasis in the stifling rift valley. It was a welcome relief to any traveler to see Jericho with its luxurious growth of verdant foliage after a hot and dusty trip.

Surely Elisha would be willing to stay there—but, of course, he was not.

As you continue to walk with God, He will give you the wisdom and understanding to overcome great obstacles that have stopped others. When He does, you should thank Him, but refuse to stay there, no matter how dramatic the victory. There are other conquests that await you. God will be with you at the next point of opposition just as He was with you at the last one. Keep on pressing forward and taking territory for your King. Don't stop at Jericho.

JORDAN

The next destination on their journey was the Jordan River. The Jordan was historically a boundary, and it meant that those who crossed were willing to leave everything behind for a desired, but uncertain, outcome. When Israel came from the wilderness, crossing the river would take them into enemy-held territory—a place where there was the possibility of danger and opposition, but also a place where opportunity abounded.

If there were ever a place for Elisha to say goodbye to his mentor, Jordan would have been the most likely spot. But it was not to be so.

Elijah wrapped his mantle together, struck the river and watched it part so both of them could cross without getting their feet wet.

It was only after they crossed that Elijah turned to his understudy and—seeing his determination to stay with

117

him—asked Elisha what he wanted. It was then Elisha asked for a double portion of Elijah's spirit to be upon him.

SERVICE POSITIONS YOU TO RECEIVE

It is amazing to me how many make it all the way to this place in their lives, and then turn aside. This is no time to become complacent—the really good things are about to begin. The doubters have been left behind. The field is wide open. Anything is possible. Now you can ask what you will, and have confidence that you are asking right, and your prayers will be rewarded.

There has been much discussion in the body of Christ about how what has become known as a *transference of anointing* actually happens. Dr. Lester Sumrall related how, through the years, many young men would come to him and ask him to lay his hands on them, so they could receive what he had. He would invariably tell them, "I don't know you. You haven't been with me. It would do neither of us any good for me to lay my hands on you. You haven't met the requirements."[8] That privilege was reserved for those with enough maturity and perseverance to pursue a genuine relationship that would benefit both generations.

Dr. Sumrall received an anointing for what would become a worldwide ministry from two of his remarkable mentors—Dr. Howard Carter and Smith Wigglesworth.

His journey with Dr. Carter is well-documented in his book *Adventuring with Christ*. What he did not have the opportunity to tell about in that volume, though, was the father-son type of relationship that developed between them during their journey. As Dr. Carter's traveling companion and helper, and because of the closeness of their relationship, he was in a position to receive a significant impartation from his mentor and friend.

Dr. Sumrall often visited Smith Wigglesworth during his stay in England before the beginning of World War II. It was at their last meeting that the former plumber and renowned evangelist wrapped his arms around the young Lester Sumrall and wept over him as he prayed for the same faith that he had to be transferred to Dr. Sumrall, as someone representing a younger generation. Dr. Sumrall later said:

"I continued to go to Wigglesworth's house about every ten days for two years. I continued to listen to him read the Word and pray, and I heard personally of the mighty miracles God had done for him around the world."[9]

It always seemed strange to him that more young men wouldn't seek to serve such a man of great faith and proven ministry as Smith Wigglesworth. Dr. Sumrall observed:

"In the two years that we had fellowship, however, I never met another visitor at his house. Nor did I ever hear him say, 'So and so was here yesterday, or will be here tomorrow.' Never once did he mention anyone visiting him."[10]

Jesus told His disciples in Luke 22:28: *"You are those who have continued with Me in My trials."*

119

Sheepdogs Among the Flock

It was only then that they heard the following words, from verses 29-30:

And I appoint to you a kingdom as My Father has appointed one to Me, so that you may eat and drink at My table in My kingdom, and sit on thrones judging the twelve tribes of Israel.

They walked with Him. They served Him. They received from Him. They were trained and made ready for ministry by His teaching and example. They were promised a heavenly reward—and they surely received it, except for the one who was disqualified because of his betrayal of his Lord and Master.

Here we see an incontrovertible truth of ministry—before the throne comes the towel—the universal sign of service. You will never sit in a seat of authority until you are willing to serve in a place of obscurity.

I remember how I started in ministry—that is, full-time ministry—the kind from which you make a living. I had moved my family to the city from a small town and was helping an evangelist and Bible teacher who rented a facility for regular meetings. I had been involved getting the building ready and was tasked with setting up chairs that we borrowed from a local church with whom we had a long-term relationship.

During the first meeting, there were over one hundred people in a small storefront building praising God and experiencing His presence. I was acting as an usher—greeting people and helping them find seats — and generally having a wonderful time when someone came up to me and said, "The toilet is plugged."

The space we were renting was long and narrow, with a workroom in the back that housed all the mechanical equipment and one very small bathroom, with only a toilet and a sink. I didn't have to inquire which toilet it was, since there was only one in the building. I knew it was operational before the meeting began, so I could only assume that some suffering saint had been delivered of their heavy burden shortly after the service started.

I distinctly remember thinking, "Hmm. The toilet's plugged. Someone should do something about that." It didn't take long to realize that someone was me.

Plumbing was not and is not my calling. I have no anointing for it whatsoever. If water runs through it and I try to fix it, it will surely become worse before it becomes better — if it becomes better at all. But none of this spared me from having to deal with the toilet at that moment.

Upon entering the bathroom, I instantly saw (and smelled) the problem. I have never seen a more thoroughly plugged toilet before or since. I was wearing church clothes, and I had nothing but a short-handled plunger — not even rubber gloves. It took multiple flushes, but through the power of prayer and the creative application of the plunger, I prevailed over the plug.

I don't remember ever getting the chance to preach in that building, but I did make sure the plumbing fixtures were functional for every service we held there. Everyone's path is different, but for me, the journey to the pulpit began at the toilet.

In asking for the double portion, Elisha was not asking Elijah for something for which he was not qualified. He had walked with the prophet for many years and had served him well and seen much in that time. He had been doing more than just watching Elijah: he had been learning and internalizing the lessons from what he heard and saw. He was ready to receive, but he was not finished.

The Bible tells us in 2 Kings 2:7 that fifty of the sons of the prophets saw the two men as they walked and talked together. They stood far off to watch what would happen. They knew that something of importance was about to take place between Elijah and Elisha, but they were neither willing nor able to follow them across the Jordan River. That privilege was reserved solely for the one who had distinguished himself by serving faithfully and without hesitation.

PICKING UP THE MANTLE

Even though the sons of the prophets knew something was coming, there was no way to know exactly when it would happen. As they watched, a flaming chariot and horses of fire appeared and Elijah was taken up by a whirlwind into heaven. Elisha was overcome, either by surprise or emotion or both, and rent his clothes and cried out in verse 12, *"My father, my father, the chariot of Israel and its horsemen!"*

Single Mantle, Double Anointing

As he looked up into the heavens after his departed mentor, counselor and friend, he saw something floating back to the ground. It was Elijah's mantle—the cloak that distinguished him as a prophet. He wouldn't need it any longer; he was leaving it behind. It landed a short distance away from his successor.

What happened next is of utmost importance. Elisha didn't just walk away from the scene. He went over, picked up Elijah's mantle and took it with him as he made his way back to the Jordan River. He struck the water as he had seen his master do, and the river parted for him just as it had for Elijah. The sons of the prophets who were watching recognized that the same spirit that had been upon Elijah was now upon Elisha.

Elijah departed from earth to heaven, but the mantle he wore, the symbol of his ministry and the anointing that made it possible, remained behind. I believe that the anointing of the Holy Spirit is like matter—it may be changed, but it cannot be destroyed.

There is no doubt that God intends people to be given as gifts to the body of Christ, and by extension, to the world. He is looking for willing vessels to carry His anointing and make His power available to those in need. Nothing can be accomplished without the activity and operation of the Holy Spirit and His enabling power.

It is important that we make a distinction between the gift and the recipient of the gift. We don't receive gifts because of who we are. If we could earn a gift, it would no longer be a gift. And like a gift that doesn't wear out or become obsolete here on earth, it can be regifted again and again.

A powerfully anointed preacher may leave the earth and go to his heavenly reward, but what happens to his mantle? What becomes of the anointing that rested on his life and ministry? There's no need for it in heaven. I believe it falls to the earth, where it awaits appropriation by someone who has been prepared to receive it, pick it up and use it.

Who knows how many life-changing—indeed, nation-changing—mantles are still lying dormant upon the earth where they fell? Who has been prepared and instructed by exercise, and is ready to pick them up and move forward to accomplish great things? What a tragic loss it has been that so many great leaders of past generations had no one positioned to pick up their mantle and continue to do exploits for the kingdom of God.

This means that often, younger ministers who come after them will have to start from the beginning and make their way in ministry, when they could have received a head start from someone who walked the path ahead of them.

Is it possible to pick up the mantle of someone whose ministry ended long ago? Look at the life and ministry of John the Baptist. He also walked in the spirit and the power of Elijah and had the same effect. He proclaimed the truth to multitudes. He made kings tremble. He turned the hearts of the fathers to the children, and the hearts of the children to their fathers. He was not one of Elijah's contemporaries, but he had his spirit. Who can tell how often this has happened, or when it will happen again?

Elijah's mantle didn't fall upon Elisha—Elisha had to go pick it up. What a tragedy it would have been had he traveled all that distance with Elijah, only to turn away, leaving the mantle behind, wading or swimming back across Jordan to continue his ministry. No—he picked it up. He was prepared, positioned and bold enough to do so. It was not disrespectful to Elijah for his successor to use the mantle that had served the elder prophet so well during his life and ministry. It would have been disrespectful to leave it lying there in the dust. Elisha's ministry from that point on demonstrated that he truly had received the double portion for which he asked.

The sons of the prophets had enabling power available to them, but it wasn't the same measure that was reserved for Elisha. He was the one who was willing to go the distance to get what he wanted and what God wanted for him.

If you are the one ordained by God to fill your leader's shoes or wear his mantle, God will make that clear, not only to you, but to your leader. But whatever your calling and ministry is, pursue it until it is realized. Don't stop at Jordan.

CHAPTER 10

An Example to the Flock

Sheep must be led, not driven. They always follow a leader—they are created that way. They never respond well to rough handling, shouting or being chased or struck. They are easily frightened and easily wounded. They don't like lots of noise or strange people or animals intruding on their domain. Any sudden or dramatic change in routine can cause them to be stressed.

A friend of ours had a beautiful country home in the middle of several acres of lush green lawn. She got tired of spending so much time mowing, so she decided to build a fence and pasture her sheep in front of her house, so they could keep the grass clipped between her home and the highway. Her experiment seemed like a great idea, except that the sheep were so afraid of the traffic on the busy road that they spent all their time huddled at the fence nearest the house.

STAY STEADY

Sheepdogs need to remember that these characteristics apply to God's sheep, too. The leaders who produce the best results are those who project quiet confidence. When trouble arises, the sheep look to those in leadership to see what they are doing. If they appear untroubled, the sheep will remain calm, but if the leaders are nervous, the sheep will be jumpy.

When trouble comes, or rumors abound, you owe it to the sheep to remain steady. If people ask you questions about what is going on, reply with confidence, even if you don't feel confident. They will take their cues from your behavior and will look to you as a stabilizing influence. I have had numerous occasions where people have come up to me after a crisis (or even during one) and said, "We didn't know what was going on, but you just kept doing things the way you always have, and we knew everything was going to be all right."

There were times when I didn't know if everything was going to be all right, but I didn't tell them that. This is a fundamental principle of leadership: never let them see you sweat. Put another way, it goes like this: act like you know what you are doing, even if you don't. It can be said even more succinctly: fake it 'til you make it.

I don't advocate deception as a leadership principle, but you must not talk about your doubts and fears among the sheep. Keep those things to yourself, and talk to God about them. If you absolutely have to talk to another human, speak to your shepherd. You would be amazed at how he can put things in perspective for you when you are being tempted to give in to doubt and fear.

During an especially nail-biting 1992 NCAA Eastern Regional Final basketball tournament game, the trailing team got the ball with just 2.1 seconds left in overtime. They were behind by one point, and their coach called a time out. He conferred with his players for a few moments, and they promptly went out and made the game-winning shot just before time expired. Afterward, sports fans wanted to know what the coach had told his players during that last time out.

"We're gonna win."[11]

He may have had just as many doubts as the fan in the thirty-fifth row, but he didn't let his players see anything but absolute confidence. That confidence inspired his players to perform up to and even beyond their capability. We need to provide the same kind of leadership to those who are watching us, especially in times of adversity.

SOMEBODY IS WATCHING YOU

It's easy to see why people would look to the pastor in times of crisis or conflict, but ministry helpers should realize that people will also look to them. In fact, your response as a helper in a time of crisis may be more important and influential than that of a pastor or other leader. This may seem counterintuitive, but let me tell you why it is true in many cases.

People will figure that the pastor will put a bold face on circumstances regardless of what comes, because he is ultimately responsible for the success or failure of every ministry endeavor. They expect him to maintain a good confession of faith, even in the most troubled times.

It's not that folks in the church won't believe or don't want to believe the pastor's demeanor or testimony of faith, it's just that they need confirmation that things are going to be all right. The ministry helpers are the next in line to receive scrutiny from the members of the flock in times like this. That's why your response is so important and so carefully watched for signs of agreement or disagreement. As a faithful sheepdog, you are the example that can confirm the words and actions of those in leadership and bring peace to the hearts of those in the church.

When the pastor casts vision, you are the first one to demonstrate your agreement. When a prayer need is mentioned, you lift your voice to pray in faith. When a deadline is set, you affirm it can be reached. When a project is unveiled, your enthusiasm is evident. When a financial goal is announced, your support is without reservation.

Here's another reason this is so vital: people may not always be able to see the pastor, but they are always able to see you, because you are among them on a regular basis. Your reaction—or lack of it—will have a considerable influence on the responses of other people in the church and even out of it. Whether you realize it or not, people are watching you. They're not just observing you casually, either—they're watching you like a hawk watches a rabbit.

An Example to the Flock

When bird dogs hunt together in the field, they range some distance from the hunters to find their quarry. If one dog locates game before the others do, it will point to indicate where the bird is hiding. Other dogs that have been properly trained will see what the other dog is doing, and even though they don't smell the bird themselves, they will quickly lock up on point, all headed in the same direction. An untrained or undisciplined dog will continue to move around indiscriminately, and if not brought to a halt, will flush the bird before the hunters are in position, ruining their chances to bag the game.

Ministry is not the equivalent of a quail hunt, but as sheepdogs, when we see the shepherd pointing in a certain direction, we ought to have as much sense as the bird dogs do and point toward the same goal. If we are uncertain or indecisive, it will cause those watching us to wonder if we are really committed to the same goal as the pastor. If they see or suspect hesitation or indecision, they will begin to have concerns about whether it is really a worthy goal or not.

We may not have the same perspective about the goal that the pastor does, but whatever goal he sets should receive our unqualified support. Others will see what we are doing and recognize that there is something going on that requires their support.

This will certainly make a difference in the church, and it can also have an enormous impact out in the marketplace.

Sheepdogs Among the Flock

If people who are unfamiliar with a local church hear something negative about it, they may be tempted to repeat it to everyone they can find. This rumor mongering will be mitigated when they have the opportunity to meet and interact with a ministry helper who is a nice and normal enough person. It will be more difficult for the gossipers to appear credible when they have a flesh and blood representative of the church they are trying to smear standing in front of them.

One ministry helper I knew worked as part of a construction crew building houses and apartments. Everyone with whom he worked knew of the dramatic changes in his life since his salvation. During a lunch break one day he overheard one of the crew members talking about his church in less than complimentary terms. He got up from where he was sitting, walked over to the gossiper and told him he was a member of that church, and the things he was saying were not true. He never heard any more lies about his church while working there. A wise man said it this way: "The man with an experience is never at the mercy of the man with an argument."

Helpers must understand that an additional measure of observation is inevitable any time they step up to assist in any area. You may be the last and least member of a one hundred voice choir, but you automatically have additional credibility in the eyes of the congregation the moment you put on the robe or take your place in the choir loft.

An Example to the Flock

You may have no other responsibility than your position as a greeter or nursery worker, but to those you serve, you represent the entire ministry, as well as the kingdom of God. If you wear a deacon's badge or an usher's jacket, you need to be mindful that those you serve see you differently than you probably see yourself.

This means that your responses, or lack thereof, will be interpreted by those around you with an additional measure of scrutiny. If everyone is saying "Amen," and you're saying nothing, people will think you are not in agreement. If others are attentive and you are unfocused, they will get the impression that what is happening doesn't matter to you. If you are late or don't show up at all, church members will use that as an opportunity to justify their tardiness or absence. You are a leader whether or not you recognize it— and what you do or don't do will provide an example for those who follow.

It's Not Just About Having a Title

There is an issue that has caused no end of grief in ministries: titles. It can be helpful to be able to call someone by a certain title to distinguish them and what they do from others who may do similar things or fulfill similar roles. We need to take care that giving someone a title is not simply a reward or something that gives them a feeling of importance, instead of something that helps them fulfill their necessary function.

There are five ministry office gifts mentioned in Ephesians 4:11 that have titles associated with them—apostle, prophet, evangelist, pastor and teacher. All of them are important gifts given by God to the body of Christ to help the saints execute their responsibilities as ambassadors of the kingdom of light in a darkened world.

Then there are deacons, taken from Acts 6 when the apostles needed additional help to fulfill certain ministry tasks. Elders are another category and are also mentioned in several places in Acts as providing leadership in many of the New Testament churches. Bishops are discussed by Paul in his letters to Timothy and Titus. I have no problem with any of these titles. But there are some cautions I believe we would do well to heed, and some extremes associated with the improper use of titles that we should avoid.

One of the surest ways to compromise a good helper's effectiveness is to give them a title. The reason for this is that many people think that once they have a title they can throw away their towel (the symbol of service—see John 13) and expect to be served rather than continue to serve as they did before they had the title.

The reason we give people titles is to acknowledge that they fulfill a function. The title should be descriptive of some kind of service provided or labor accomplished, not an honorific that replaces any further involvement in the very things that led to the title being given in the first place.

In some churches, everyone has a title. I suppose that's all right if everyone *does* something, but I have yet to see a church where that is the case. In too many places, the 80/20 principle is in place — that is, 80 percent of the work is done by 20 percent of the people. In even more places, that ratio is more like 95/5. But the greater the percentage of people who are involved in the work of the ministry, the healthier the church body is likely to be.

Let's take the word *deacon* as an example. The term represents someone who serves. The first deacons in Acts served the widows in the daily food distribution. But today, in many cases, deacons don't serve, but expect to be served simply because they are deacons. The title should describe the function, not just the position.

Those who have earned their Ph.D. or similar graduate degrees or have had an honorary doctoral degree conferred upon them due to their accomplishments by a legitimate institution of higher learning — and call themselves *Doctor* — have my respect and my congratulations. But if someone bought their doctoral degree at a diploma mill and expects everyone to call them *Doctor* as a result, to me it diminishes the respect that the title ought to convey due to the discipline and sacrifice that has traditionally been necessary to obtain it.

Sometimes this matter of titles borders on the ridiculous. If you require those around you to call you the *Primary Potentate* and *Principal Paterfamilias* of your church or organization, who besides you or your ministry associates know (or care) what those designations actually mean? They sound impressive, but how do they assist anyone in understanding what you are to them or how you can help them?

Please don't misunderstand my intentions. Those who start and build churches have a legitimate claim to the title *Apostle*. Those who see and know things supernaturally by the revelation gifts of the Spirit as a part of their calling and ministry can call themselves prophets. Anyone who serves in some capacity in the church can wear their deacon badge all day and night if they choose. But if someone wants to be called a deacon just so they can get a seat on the front row, I have to wonder if they have any appreciation for what the historical meaning of the term is.

RESPONDING APPROPRIATELY

If you have been afforded the privilege of sitting in the front of the church, you should be one of the best and most appropriate responders in the place every time you are there. Far too often I have seen people treat any special consideration given to them in seating as a right and not a privilege, and then sit there like proverbial bumps on a log, or sometimes like toads on a toadstool while the service is being conducted. The preacher could stand on his head without getting so much as a grunt of affirmation out of them.

Every church has different expectations when it comes to responding to the preaching or teaching. You may not be accustomed to clapping your hands or shouting in your church. But even if your services are on the quiet end of the spectrum, those behind the pulpit will always appreciate even a little bit of appropriate agreement at some point.

A friend told me about conducting a service among some people who had recently come out of a rather formal church organization. One man in particular caught his attention—not because of his abundance of enthusiasm, but because of his lack of it. This fellow sat on the front row and never moved during the entire ministry portion of the service. He scarcely blinked. The preacher thought he was surely not getting through to him.

After the service as my friend stood at the door greeting people while they left the building, this man came up and congratulated him on his preaching. "I just want you to know," the man said, "that was the most inspiring message I've heard in all my life."

"I'm glad he was inspired," my friend said. "If the message had been boring, he might have quit breathing."

In any case, ministry helpers, regardless of what they are called, ought to be enthusiastic in their support for the vision, the preaching, the praise and anything else that may elicit a response. Other sheep around you will observe and follow your example.

IT'S ABOUT FORMING RELATIONSHIPS

If you are a ministry helper, when you are in attendance, you should be helping and serving, not waiting for an opportunity to be served. At church functions, you should not only be in attendance, but be moving among the others who are there—greeting them, talking to them, asking about their welfare and generally spending time with them. I have seen staff members or helpers who already know one another get into their own small groups and spend all their time talking to one another. This defeats one of the prime purposes for these kinds of fellowships, which is to get to know those who attend and develop relationships with them.

Unless you are designated to stay in a certain place or have a certain set of responsibilities that prevent you from doing so, get out there among the sheep and make your presence known. Give a word of encouragement to someone who needs it. Shake hands. Smile. Introduce yourself. Listen to a few testimonies, or just the stories that people want to share with you. Ask about their families. This is all a part of the serving process. It is also how relationships are built and strengthened in a local body of believers.

A church is not a building. It is not an organization or a denomination. A church is people, and the relationships those people develop with one another over time, and as a result of shared experiences. When relationships between individuals are strengthened, a church cannot help but be strengthened. This, too, is a vital part of the helper's ministry.

You may not think of it in these terms, but every time you go to the foyer to greet people, you are building the church. When you reach out to people during a time of crisis in their lives, it is a church-building exercise. Your presence and your smile doesn't just make you better, it makes the body of believers of which you are a part better. Don't neglect this aspect of ministry. It is simple, but powerful. People will watch you and emulate your acts of hospitality and kindness, which will help them, as well as those with whom they interact.

Stephen served tables, but that's not all he did. Acts 6:8 says he did great wonders and miracles among the people. While he was taking a widow her plate of food, he had the opportunity to ask how she was getting along and pray for her on the spot. No doubt he also prayed for many others who received answers to their prayers right then. This is also a part of your service. No act of kindness given with a pure motive is insignificant. Jesus said something as small as a cup of cold water given in His name would result in a heavenly reward.

Your example is a powerful witness wherever you are. People will watch you to make sure your life outside the walls of the church lines up with your profession inside the church. Your consistent example provides a well-defined and straight path for the sheep to follow.

My wife and I were in a big box store talking to a sales representative about a new appliance—it may have been a washer or dryer. By the time we had been there ten minutes, no less than three different people came up to us and greeted us warmly, as though they knew us—because they did—from church. After the third such greeting, the salesperson stood back, looked us up and down and said, "Who are you?"

He thought we must surely be celebrities or people he should recognize, since it seemed like everyone else did. This type of recognition out in the community doesn't come from a title given within the church. It comes from countless interactions with people that cause relationships to develop and carry on outside the walls of the church.

I was telling a church member about this incident later, and she laughed and said, "Elder Canfield, you're always representing." It's true. Faithful sheepdogs are always representing—their pastor, their church and their Lord. Don't be afraid to smell like sheep—get out there among them and love them and care for them. You are an example to the flock.

CHAPTER 11

The Shepherd's Thing, Not Your Thing

A world famous children's author wrote a book in which a boy who visited the zoo dreamed about all the changes he would make if he were in charge. Of course, he wasn't in charge, so the zoo just kept running the way it always had.

Regardless of how faithful or respectful they may be, sheepdogs may sometimes want to do things differently than the way the shepherd has directed. It can be tempting at times to play the "If I Were the Shepherd" game.

I have some helpful advice for all helpers: you are not the shepherd. You are supposed to be helping the shepherd, so help him—don't try to supplant him or become his substitute. Use this guideline when you have received instructions: do it, do it right away, and do it the way the shepherd wants it done.

Sheepdogs Among the Flock

A GOOD IDEA OR A GOD IDEA?

Just because you have a good idea doesn't mean it is a God idea. Abraham discovered this when he attempted to assist God in producing an heir. God's plan created Isaac. Abraham's plan resulted in Ishmael. Lots of good ideas have come to bad ends, not because they weren't good ideas, but because their time had not come or the resources necessary for their implementation were not available. If you pitch an idea to your leader, and he doesn't approve it, don't trouble yourself about it any longer. Just because he hasn't approved your *idea* is no indication he doesn't approve of *you*.

Have you ever seen a situation where the pastor didn't really want something to happen, but it happened anyway, just because someone else had an idea and pressed the matter so insistently? Here's an example of this.

A church was growing rapidly, and people from neighboring communities were coming in increasing numbers. Some of them had transportation issues, so someone suggested that the church get a bus to transport them. The pastor said no, because the Lord never said anything to him about a bus ministry. The person who wanted it to happen spoke to some other people about it, and a groundswell of support began to percolate among the congregation.

A driver volunteered. A potential vehicle was located, and negotiations to purchase it began. This all happened without the pastor's knowledge, so when he found out about it, he asked for a meeting with the leaders of this fledgling bus movement.

Proponents painted rosy scenarios of how much the church would benefit. They gave detailed descriptions of busloads of happy folks who would otherwise not have the opportunity to come to the church who would be attending every week. Financial issues were examined, and assurances were made.

They finally convinced the pastor of the soundness of their plan. Against his better judgment, he told them to go ahead, figuring he could cut his losses and use the bus for other purposes if things didn't work out as described. The bus contingent was elated.

The church bought the bus, which was a short version of the yellow 66-passenger school buses that are such a common sight in communities everywhere. It cost more than was budgeted for it, which was only a harbinger of things to come. Next, it had to pass a state inspection before it could be used. New tires and an exhaust system that needed to be replaced were additional expenses, since the bus had about a million miles on it and had not been well-maintained by the previous owner. Finally, it was ready to roll.

The first week the bus ran its route in the nearby community, it came into the church parking lot full of people who were laughing and rejoicing as they came into the church. It looked like the beginning of a successful bus ministry after all. This continued week after week—until...

Sheepdogs Among the Flock

The number of people riding the bus began to diminish, for reasons unknown. Soon the bus was only half full. Then it only had a handful of riders. Part of the pitch the bus proponents had made was that the people coming to church on the bus would give offerings which would more than make up for the expense. That didn't happen, and it didn't take long for the bus ministry to become a hole into which the church poured money, with no bottom in sight.

The reasons for this failure are numerous and complex. Suffice it to say it was a good idea, but not God's idea. It was an expensive lesson, but one that had value nonetheless.

You may have lots of worthy ideas, but regardless of how good they sound, if you don't have the agreement of your pastor, you shouldn't spend ministry time and money chasing them. Chances are you don't have better ideas than the person God put in charge. If that were the case, you would be the one in charge. As a helper, that's not your place. Your place is to fulfill the order, not to place the order.

There are two errors that helpers can make in following orders, and both are equally damaging. The first is to do things before receiving proper authorization. If the shepherd says to wait, a faithful helper will wait, regardless of how urgent the situation may seem. The well-trained soldier holds his fire until he hears the appropriate command from his superiors. Feel free to take matters into your own hands only if the matters belong to you. Otherwise, that course of action will seldom lead to the desired result.

The Shepherd's Thing, Not Your Thing

The second error is delayed obedience, which is often the equivalent of disobedience. Regardless of how distasteful a task may seem, if it has been ordered, it must be done. Problems won't go away by themselves—they tend to metastasize and grow bigger through neglect. Astute shepherds know this, which is why they have given you directions to address the situation. If you are called to be a helper, you'll be busy enough fulfilling that set of responsibilities without looking for more.

YOU DON'T WANT TO BE IN CHARGE

Not long after I began attending the church where I work, someone asked me if I ever wanted to pastor my own church. I told him not to get that kind of talk started. I am not called to be a pastor, and I didn't want anyone assuming that I was just because I was on the church staff. Even though I have never pastored a church, I have never felt unfulfilled or unsatisfied in ministry. Despite what you may have experienced, not everyone who helps a pastor is secretly longing for the day when they get to be in charge.

Here's another piece of advice: you really don't want to be the shepherd. Being in the top position is overrated. Lots of people want the lights, the platform and the microphone, but they don't recognize the responsibilities that go along with those things. If they did, they wouldn't be so eager to be in charge.

There will be those who come alongside to help who are genuinely called to go on and pastor after a period of proven apprenticeship. They can learn how to do much of what they will need to do by helping another pastor. But I believe God is raising up many others all over the world whose ultimate assignment is to assist a pastor in fulfilling the vision God gave him.

Even though sheepdogs share the responsibilities of leadership, their measure of that responsibility is a fraction of what the shepherd carries every day. I can go home at night without having to worry about the building program, the church finances, whether the roof is leaking, whether the parking lots need cleared of snow, or about the volunteers who can't get along between departments—or sometimes even within the same department. That doesn't mean I close up the office every day at 4:55 pm and forget about everything else, but as a helper I simply don't have the burden on me that the shepherd has on him.

Something that has always amazed me is how people tend to think that things have always been the way they are right now. They see the lights, the cameras, and the action, and are convinced that the church just came down from heaven fully formed without any effort or sacrifice. There is a risk associated with every reward, and the crucifixion came before the resurrection. A seed must be sown to reap a harvest. People may see the harvest of what they perceive is a successful ministry, but they don't realize the seeds that were sown or the labor that was necessary to see that harvest come to fruition.

Most of the work of ministry does not take place on the platform or from behind the pulpit. Platform or pulpit time, in many ways, is the reward preachers get for doing the other work that needs to be done.

Anyone who thinks ministry is glamorous is unfamiliar with it. Much of what ministry really is takes place behind the closed doors of a prayer closet, where there are no bright lights and no sound systems, just the light of heaven and the sound of God's voice.

The apostle Paul, in discussing what it means to be a minister of Christ in 2 Corinthians 11, spoke of being imprisoned, beaten, stoned, shipwrecked, hungry, thirsty and in a continual state of fasting for the cause of Christ. In addition to this, he said that the care and concern for the welfare of not just one church, but all the churches he oversaw, came upon him daily. He was conveying the fact that overseeing a ministry was a daily process, one that never ended and needed constant attention.

That is one reason why many are called, and few are chosen. Many are excited about starting, but relatively few remain until they cross the finish line.

Here's another principle to remember: if you want to see the rainbow, there has to be rain. Things won't always be bright and cheery. You will go through some dark days and some dreary times, but don't allow discouragement to disenchant you. The earth will turn, and darkness will give way to dawn once again. Keep on pressing toward your goal. You may not be able to sprint, but crawl if you can't do anything else. If you don't have enough strength to crawl, God will reward you if you just lean in the right direction.

WHAT IF I DON'T AGREE?

Here's an issue that will inevitably arise between shepherds and those who help them: what do you do as a sheepdog when the shepherd tells you to do something with which you don't agree?

My rule of conduct and advice to all ministry helpers is this: if you are asked to do it, you should do it. There are a few exceptions to this, but most of the time, you should just do it. Let me explain why.

The ultimate responsibility for whatever is done does not belong to you. It belongs to the pastor. We should respect the authority of the office and recognize that all authority eventually comes from God. God Himself instituted delegated authority, and if He trusts men enough to give them authority, we should trust Him enough to obey it, regardless of whether we agree with it. God didn't ever tell His people that they should obey if they understood, or if they agreed. He just told them to obey. Our blessing is in our obedience, not in our understanding.

No comparison between God and men is perfect, because God is perfect, and men are not. But the matter of obedience to authority is a controversy that predates human history. We will never be able to fulfill God's purpose if we don't get this matter straight in our hearts and our minds.

And to help us do just that, God gives us delegated authority.

The problems that arise in this area seldom have to do with direct authority—that is, instructions that come from God Himself. Even the most difficult and obtuse of His servants will generally acknowledge that God's commands are not optional and not flexible. Where the challenge is greatest is when delegated authority—God's representative—gives direction, and those under that authority find a myriad of reasons to either take some other sort of action or no action at all. We may call them reasons, but in reality, they are often nothing more than excuses.

1 Samuel 15:22-23 says:

Obedience is better than sacrifice, a listening ear than the fat of rams. For rebellion is as the sin of witchcraft, and stubbornness is as iniquity and idolatry.

This doesn't just refer to instructions we receive from God Himself—it refers to His directives, regardless of who gives them. Saul received the word to destroy the Amalekites through the prophet Samuel, not from God Himself. He respected Samuel enough to at least say he was going to fulfill the word of the Lord—even though he did not do it. What would Saul's response have been if he had received that directive from someone he did not respect?

In matters of direction from delegated authority, personalities must be disregarded so we can attend to the more pressing matter of obedience to God. This is generally not a problem when it comes to dealing with the pastor, but it is more likely to be an issue when dealing with someone who is under the pastor. But the same principle regarding delegated authority applies. You may not like the person giving you direction, and you may not choose to spend time in fellowship with them. They may not be your best friend, but you are obligated to follow their instructions when they are representing authority.

Here are some guidelines that will help you in this area.

If there is a problem that will compromise the completion of a direction that you have been given, say so, and say it right away. It may be information that is necessary for the pastor to know. Good decisions can't be made with bad information. But don't just resist the directive because it is unsavory to you. If you have a question about directions that are unclear, ask up front, but don't use questions as a reason to delay or deny the inevitable.

If you can't do something, have a legitimate reason for not doing it. If your deadline is next week, and you're on vacation next week, speak up. Adjustments are more easily made ahead of time than when facing a drop-dead date (usually with emphasis on the dead part).

However, there are those who raise innumerable objections simply because they don't want to fulfill the task. Some people work harder at shirking than they do at working. These aren't the ones you want on your team, and your pastor doesn't want them on his team, either.

The Shepherd's Thing, Not Your Thing

Instead of offering excuses, offer suggestions. Give a solution for how it *can* be done instead of a reason why it *can't* be done. Look at alternatives in addition to consequences. Think the matter through to its conclusion. Ask the next question, not just the first one. But at all times and in all circumstances, remember: you are not the shepherd.

A submitted heart will reveal itself in all matters of importance, but there is one sure way to know if you are with your leader in spirit. It is not how you respond when everything is going well, and you are experiencing the favor and blessing of your pastor that demonstrates your commitment. It is how you deal with being corrected or being told to do something that seems unnecessary and even irritating to you. Obedience in this circumstance is where the loyalty of the subordinate is truly proven.

IS DISOBEDIENCE EVER ACCEPTABLE?

Is there ever a time when you should refuse to do what you are asked or directed to do? Before answering this question, you must first examine your heart and be absolutely convinced that the reason for your refusal is not just because you don't want to do it. This requires integrity before God and men.

Adam chose to be less than honest with God in Genesis chapter 3, and it has led to consequences for all of his progeny. Be forthright with yourself and with your leaders. The pain of completing a formidable and forbidding responsibility will be far less grievous than the alternatives — for you and for others.

There are only three instances where you cannot comply with requests that are made of you, and they are these: when you are asked to do something that is immoral, illegal or unethical.

The first question that arises upon seeing this list is why a person in authority would ask you or require you to do any of these things. It is a fair question, and one that should cause you to seriously evaluate your relationship with someone who would put you in that position. If this happens repeatedly, it is a signal that you need to fulfill your helping ministry somewhere else.

IF IT'S IMMORAL

A young man came to me in obvious turmoil. He explained that he had a long and profitable relationship with his mentor, who had helped him through many difficult times in his life. The young man had the opportunity to accompany the older man and learn from him in many settings, both public and private. They had come to the point where they were more like a father and son in the faith, similar to Paul and Timothy — at least that is the way the young man perceived their relationship. But Paul, in 2 Timothy 2, counseled Timothy to avoid anything that would keep him from being a vessel unto honor, fit for God to use, and not to embrace ungodly things, or take part in them.

The Shepherd's Thing, Not Your Thing

One day the older man asked the young man to accompany him to a place where he had never taken him before and demanded that he do some things that were immoral—and that is putting it mildly. To his credit, the young man refused, but he was emotionally devastated. Not only was his own reputation put at risk, but he lost respect for—and his relationship with—a man he had grown to love and trust. He was absolutely correct in refusing, and he was cautioned to never again allow that person who would take advantage of his trust in such a brazen way to be near him again.

IF IT'S ILLEGAL

What should you do if you are asked to do something that is illegal?

One of the most frequent problems I have seen in this area involves traffic laws—specifically, speed limits. This may seem like a minor infraction, but a speed limit is a law nonetheless. Preachers always seem to be in a hurry—to get to church services, meetings, appointments, and a variety of other time-sensitive opportunities. When they are traveling on the streets and highways, they sometimes have an inclination to justify going faster than the law allows since they are doing such important work and have so many unforeseen distractions that keep them behind schedule, you see.

If you are driving someone who asks you to speed to get somewhere on time, you need to remember that speeding is breaking the law. If we become accustomed to lawlessness in one area, our hearts will become immune to breaking the law in another area. Before long, we risk having a conscience that is insensitive to the voice of the Spirit, and we will find ourselves in trouble that could have been avoided if we would have refused to break the law in the first place.

This may seem trivial, but it can have life-altering implications. The law where I live mandates that drivers and passengers in vehicles wear seat belts. One snowy February morning, a staff member was on his way to his office at the church. It was not his habit to wear a seat belt, but this time, he obeyed the prompting of the Holy Spirit, and put it on. He was involved in a head-on collision just around the corner from his home. The other driver was not wearing a seat belt. One of them survived the crash and is alive today — and the other one is not.

If It's Unethical

Of these three areas, questions of ethics present the greatest opportunity for misunderstanding. Although customs and methods may vary from place to place, if you have any doubt about the propriety of a course of action, it is best to choose another way to accomplish a task. If there is no other way, the ethical thing to do is to decline, politely and respectfully, but firmly. Unethical behavior should be consistently and absolutely resisted by everyone who calls himself a Christian.

Some of the biggest opportunities for temptation in this area are regarding the use of ministry money, equipment or time to deal with personal business. What belongs to the church really belongs to God. Don't allow yourself to touch it for personal purposes. If you handle money, make sure it is done with rigorous accounting. If you drive a church vehicle, don't accomplish personal errands while using it. Church computers or other pieces of equipment are for church use only. And don't forget that stealing time is still stealing. When you are at work, you need to be working on God's business, not conducting your own.

And one more thing—don't ask me to cover you by lying for you. If you were late, I will not certify that you were on time. If I don't know where you are or what you are doing, I'm not making excuses for you. I'm not going to participate in your foolishness. Resist the pressure to engage in unethical behavior at any time, for any reason.

As a faithful helper, you will not be looking for ways not to do what you are asked to do by your leaders. You will be seeking—and finding—ways to help them do what God has directed them to do under the leadership of the head of the church, the Lord Jesus Christ.

CHAPTER 12

How Can I Help
These People?

The people you have the privilege of serving do
not belong to you. They do not belong to your
pastor, either. They belong to God, and you will
ultimately answer to Him about how you deal with them. If
you care about God, you will care about His people and will
treat them with the same deference and dedication that you
expect to receive as one of God's people yourself.

The people you serve are precious to Him. We have ir-
refutable evidence of this, because He sent His Son to die for
them. How much more should we be willing to live for
them?

Recent headlines confirm that there are those in ministry who do not care for God's flock, but only for their own
well-being. The Old Testament prophets—such as Jeremiah—had some scathing rebukes for those who lorded
over God's heritage and did not treat His people with the
compassion that God commissioned and expected His servants to provide. (So did Peter, Paul, John, Jude and Jesus.)

Sheepdogs Among the Flock

Jeremiah 23:1-2 pronounces woe upon the pastors who destroy and scatter the sheep, declaring that they would receive the recompense of their ways for how they treated God's flock.

MINISTRY TO PEOPLE REQUIRES FOCUS AND COMPASSION

When people need ministry, they rightfully expect to be ministered to—not ignored, neglected or given less than your full attention and effort. Often, this ministry will not be from the shepherd, but from a faithful sheepdog. Ministry interactions are not the time to be distracted by other people, agendas or deadlines.

Your focus should be on the person or people in front of you—finding out about and speaking to their need. Simple steps such as looking them in the eye, shaking their hand and repeating their name go a long way toward putting them at ease and making sure they know that someone on earth cares about them, is willing to listen to them and will pray specifically about their situation.

Being a helper in ministry means that people will look to you for assistance in coming to terms with the dilemmas they face in a variety of circumstances. Sometimes caretakers of God's flock think they are always expected to have an answer for every question people have. But life doesn't always lend itself to easy answers, and there are some questions to which there are no answers, easy or otherwise. Just because you don't have a solution to a complex or particularly vexing problem doesn't mean you're not a good helper, or that God doesn't exist, or that He is indifferent to those who are hurting.

How can you explain some things that happen to people? How do you minister to a couple who believed God against all odds to have a baby, only to have that baby die of SIDS when it was five months old? What do you tell a devastated family whose teenager is dead due to a self-inflicted gunshot wound, a drug overdose or an automobile accident? What words will adequately explain the purpose of God to a woman whose husband walked out on her after more than twenty years of marriage? How will you convince a man to find a reason to keep on living after his life-long companion and the love of his life for over fifty years of marriage died suddenly and unexpectedly?

What about the parents who are struggling to understand why their only daughter died of AIDS, when nobody, including her husband, knew she was infected before they were married? Can you explain why the son who was raised in a home where love and respect were not just preached, but practiced, and who loved his parents, loved God, and loved church, has renounced everything he believed to be true, and has become the antithesis of what he was?

What will you say in these cases, and many others like them? Will you point a finger of condemnation at the people who have questions about these experiences? Can you confidently say it is their sin or their parents' sin that caused the heartache they are now experiencing? Do you dare resort to some unhelpful and untrue bromide such as, "God has plucked another flower for His heavenly garden"?

Will you give them a pat answer and a pat on the back, pray a little prayer and go your way without giving them another thought? Will you just shrug your shoulders and say, "I don't know the answer," leaving them without any measure of comfort that they desperately need?

We know that we live in a fallen world—at least we should know it from reading the Bible. If that doesn't convince us, a cursory glance around our culture at a world in turmoil should do it. Bad things happen to good people, but that is not proof that God is not the good, gracious, merciful and caring God we see in His Word. But knowing this in our heads may not help us when our hearts are overwhelmed with grief, anger or some other emotion that is part of the human condition. How can those of us in a helping role bring peace to a life that has been turned upside down?

WHAT HAPPENS WHEN YOU HAVE NO ANSWERS?

One of the worst things you can do in situations like these is to try to make some kind of excuse for what you don't know, or for what seems like God's distance from those who are suffering. I can't begin to tell you how many people have been turned away from God by some well-meaning but misinformed person telling them that God took their loved one, or that God has a purpose, but we don't know what it is, or maybe it is better this way. I'm sure we've all heard these kinds of opinions—hopefully, we have not disseminated them.

I tell people who have suffered a tragic loss that they should be ready for people to tell them all sorts of things. Often, folks who encounter those who are grieving are uncomfortable not saying anything, so they say whatever they can think of, and sometimes it is not helpful.

In times of distress and grief, you don't really have to say anything—just your presence can be a source of comfort. I don't recommend Job's friends as role models, but they did know how to sit and be silent instead of filling the room with blather as soon as they came in.

Don't try to come up with cute little phrases that are generic in nature and do more harm than good. You can't explain everything, and you shouldn't try. Don't guess if you don't know.

There is a tremendous temptation at times like these to ask the question, "Why?" Sometimes—perhaps many times—you won't know why, and you should be honest enough to say so, but don't just leave it at that.

When I was a kid, there was a marsh with acres of cattails in it near my home. My cousin and I thought it would be fun to put on hip boots and go walking through it. In some places, even though the water was shallow, the muck underneath was three feet deep, and we would sink in above our knees. There was not much room for error in a place like that, because every effort to extract one foot would drive the other foot deeper, and getting cold, muddy water in your hip boots was a nasty business. At those times, we had enough sense to turn around and go back to solid ground.

There will be times in ministry when we are on uncertain ground. On those occasions, we need to have enough sense to stop moving forward into uncharted territory and turn around and go back to what is more familiar. When you get to the place where you don't know the answers and are unsure what to tell someone, go back to solid ground.

What you know for certain at that moment may not be much more than "Jesus loves you," or "God is still alive." You may have to leave the "why" questions unanswered. Some problems may defy adequate explanations. But even in that circumstance, there is peace available from a gracious and omniscient God.

Here is something that happened to me as I was considering a "why" question of my own. I was complaining to God about not knowing the answer to a certain situation when the Holy Spirit spoke to me very calmly and quietly.

"Leave that to Me," He said.

"No, God," I said in all of my wisdom. "I want to know why!"

"You are better off not knowing," God said.

"I want to know why, and I want to know now!" I demanded.

After a moment, God answered. "What if I told you it was your fault?" He said. "What if it was because you did not pray when I prompted you, did not speak when I commanded you, and did not repent when I required you to repent? Do you really want to know if you were responsible for what happened? Can you deal with that?"

"No, God," I said.

"Then be obedient, and leave the rest to Me," God said.

When I was young, it was customary for my grandfather, who lived with us, to sit on the sofa after dinner to watch the evening news. It was also customary for me to get up from the dinner table and run around, contrary to my parents' instructions. Sure enough, I would get a tummy ache. I would start complaining about it, and my grandfather would tell me to come over and sit next to him on the sofa. He would put his arm around me and hold me next to him for a while. I would calm down and sit by his side, enjoying the smell of his Old Spice after shave, and the pain would go away. I couldn't explain how it happened, but it always worked. After some time, he would ask me if I felt better, and I would say I did and get up and go on my way.

I believe when people are hurting, they don't need to be told why they are hurting. What they do need is to be able to find a place near God's heart where they can find rest for their weary souls and healing for their broken hearts. As a child, I didn't need an explanation of why I had a stomach ache—I needed a safe place to rest and recover. Instruction could come later, when it could be received, but right then what I needed was a person to hold on to me until the pain no longer incapacitated me.

Sheepdogs Among the Flock

That's what we can do for people who are hurting and don't know what to do about it. That's what we can offer to those who are struggling to understand why the accident or the illness or the devastation happened. We probably won't have the answer, but we can at least hold on to them until they stop hurting and are able to regain their emotional equilibrium. That is the most valuable thing we can do.

At times like these, people don't really need answers to unanswerable questions. What they need more than anything else is God's presence. You can help provide an atmosphere where His presence can overtake them and give them hope and peace. I've seen it happen over and over again.

YOU CAN'T HELP EVERYONE, BUT YOU CAN HELP SOMEONE

I wish I could tell you it happens every time. Before you have been in ministry very long, you will discover that there are people you can't help. That does not mean they can't be helped, because Jesus has help for everyone. But there will be some who are either beyond your ability or opportunity to help, or who will not or cannot receive from you. We shouldn't throw up our hands after the first or second effort and think that it is useless to try. Sometimes our attempts fall short because we give up too soon. But when we encounter those we can't reach—whatever the reason—it doesn't mean that they are unreachable, or that we are failures.

In the parable of the sower, Jesus said there were four kinds of ground. Some ground would not receive seed at all—other kinds would have varying degrees of success. People move through different seasons of life. Sometimes their hearts may be like stony ground, or even like the wayside, where the seed cannot take root. But at another time, that same person may be good ground. Don't allow yourself to become discouraged because you don't always see the results you expect from your efforts at helping. One lesson of the parable of the sower is to be diligent in sowing seed. The more seed you sow, the greater the harvest you will reap.

Just because you can't help everyone doesn't mean you can't help someone. Consider the little boy who was walking on the beach after a storm. Thousands of starfish were stranded, and the boy was picking up as many of them as he could and tossing them back into the ocean. An old man encountered him at his labor.

"What are you doing, son?"

"I'm putting these starfish back into the water," the boy said.

"Well, I can see that, but why? There are thousands of starfish on this beach, as far as the eye can see. What makes you think that what you're doing will make a difference?"

The little boy looked down at the starfish in his hand, and then looked up at the old man. "It'll make a difference to this one," he said, as he tossed it into the surf.[12]

Another principle that will help you in dealing with people is to focus on what you can do, not on what you can't

165

do. If you always focus on your lack, your inconsistencies and your liabilities, you will have a hard time staying encouraged. The devil will keep a comprehensive list of your failures and remind you of them on a regular basis. Don't let this stop you or keep you from making an effort to be successful.

I saw this illustrated while watching a televised World Series baseball game. One of the teams had not made it to that level for decades. The pressure that was on them to win must have been incredible. Something that was particularly frustrating to me was to see batter after batter looking at good pitches time after time instead of trying to hit them.

To hit the ball, you must swing the bat. You might miss, and you might even strike out. But as the old saying affirms, "Can't never tried." Trying and failing is better than not trying at all. Those who never make an effort to accomplish anything don't fail—but they never succeed, either. (The team that kept their bats on their shoulders lost the game and the Series.)

SOMETIMES YOU HAVE TO SAY "NO"

Another important consideration is to know your limits. Realize what you can and can't do, and don't make promises you can't keep. There is no need to apologize for not accomplishing what is beyond your capability.

There will be times in ministry when you will have to tell people *no*. You cannot be all things to all people. You must keep your priorities straight, minister to your family, follow the directions you have been given, and still go to heaven yourself. In fact, sometimes the most humane thing you can do is refuse certain requests that people make of you, and mean it, right up front.

Nearly every week, I get asked to do things I can't do, or won't do, or shouldn't do. I used to feel like I had to accommodate everyone, and I would find myself in a mess more often than not. I would have to spend more time explaining myself and apologizing to everyone involved than I would have by just refusing right away. Now, when someone asks me to do something that I am unable or unwilling to do, I simply say, "No, I can't (or won't) do that."

I am not talking about refusing legitimate requests for ministry or prayer. What I mean is feeling obligated to automatically acquiesce to every request that comes my way, regardless of how unlikely or unreasonable it is.

No, I can't provide you with a place to live. No, I won't become your taxi service, your lending institution or your best friend. No, I'm not going to interrupt the flow of a service so you can ask the pastor a question. No, I will not hand you the microphone so you can say who knows what for who knows how long. I'm willing to agree with you in prayer and stand with you in faith, but I can't do your praying or your believing for you.

If there is someone else who can help them, I will refer them. If not, I just say no. Sometimes an explanation is required, but often it is not. I don't know of anyone who has been irrevocably damaged by this approach. Try it. You may find it saves you a bundle of grief.

Sheepdogs Among the Flock

You may say, "But Jesus always granted people's requests." No, He didn't. The man who asked Him to intervene in a family matter regarding the division of an inheritance was flatly refused (see Luke 12:13-15). Matthew 20:20-23 tells of a request by Zebedee's wife that Jesus plainly said He could not grant. That didn't mean He didn't love them. Your refusal to do certain things doesn't prove that you don't love people, either.

Jesus said in John 10:11: *I am the good shepherd. The good shepherd lays down His life for the sheep.*

His words were followed by His actions as He sacrificed Himself on the altar of a cross on a hill just outside the walls of Jerusalem. Christ laid down His life for these sheep — even the ones who butt and bolt and back away — especially for them. As sheepdogs, He calls us to follow His example. How can we do less than lay down our lives as well?

THESE FOUR THINGS WILL HELP US HELP THE SHEEP

There are four characteristics that all ministry helpers need to display toward those they are helping:

1. **Patience:** Patience is a fruit of the Spirit. It is placed in us by the operation of the Holy Spirit when we are born again. We must be patient with others. They can and will change, but not always as fast as we would like. They'll get the concepts we are demonstrating eventually, but they may not assimilate them as readily or practice them in exactly the way we would hope. All of us have different abilities

and varying capacities for change. When you are tempted to become impatient with someone, remember how longsuffering God has been, and still is, with you.

2. **Perseverance:** Perseverance is the ability to endure. God's nature and character doesn't change. The way yours should change is to become more like Him. He didn't give up on you—don't give up on others. Everyone needs someone to believe in them and stick with them.

3. **Prayer:** Believing prayer will enable you to overcome any obstacle and bear any burden. Your prayer life should include a significant investment in those to whom you minister. Their breakthrough may be the result of your steadfast and regular prayer on their behalf.

4. **Peace:** Peace should be the result of our labor. The peace that comes through our faithful effort is not just the absence of external conflict, but a quiet confidence that transcends our understanding and captures and controls our hearts. This peace should extend to God's sheep over whom we watch and for whom we care. All sheep, natural and spiritual alike, thrive when they are at peace. And when the flock is at peace, it's more likely that the shepherd and all his faithful sheepdogs will experience peace, too.

CHAPTER 13

This Is My Place

One question I am frequently asked is, "How have you managed to stay at one place for so many years?" The answer is not complicated. If you know you are where you are supposed to be, doing what you are supposed to do, that will hold you steady regardless of what else happens. When other people leave, it may affect you, but it won't move you. When storm clouds and threatening winds rise, you won't feel tempted to jump overboard. Even when personal tragedy strikes, you can be confident that you are positioned to overcome it when you are in the right place for the right reasons.

ARE YOU POSITIONED FOR SUCCESS?

I'm not saying that the only possible explanation for someone leaving a ministry opportunity after a short period of time is that they are uncommitted, indecisive or have no spiritual strength or stamina. Some seasons of opportunity are brief, and people move on for a variety of legitimate reasons. I'm suggesting one common reason so many ministry helpers don't last very long is because they didn't have the confidence they were in the right place when they started, and never developed it during their time there.

You may feel that you are positioned for success in the greatest church in the world, serving the greatest pastor and the greatest people, or you may have concerns about the place you are in right now. You may be settled and content in a place where you have been for a long time (or just arrived) or looking for a way out as diligently as you looked for a way in, whether it was a decade, a year, or a month ago.

Regardless of where you are and how good or how terrible things may seem, adversity will come to you. Don't wonder about *if* it will come—it is only a matter of *when*. Whether or not you stand through it depends on the foundation upon which your spiritual house is built (see Luke 6:47-49). It is important to not be distracted when difficulties arise, because if that happens, the devil will see to it that trouble will blow you off course continually.

You may be falsely accused. Your motives may be misunderstood. You may be judged, ridiculed, shouted at or otherwise mistreated by those you give your life to serve. You may even be treated unfairly by others with whom you work. If you do your job right, you will certainly be called all sorts of unkind things. Most of the time, these accusations will not be worth the time it takes to listen to them, and you must not let them influence your behavior or your obedience.

SOMETIMES WE CAUSE OUR OWN PROBLEMS

From time to time, though, you should take an honest appraisal of your life and service to make sure you are not overlooking something that needs to be corrected. I don't recommend that we wander through life compulsively picking lint out of our navels, but we do need to allow God to give us a thorough examination and point out errors that must be made right.

Much of the adversity we encounter is not due to persecution for the sake of the gospel, or even due to the devil's activity, either directly or indirectly. Much of what we go through is related to decisions we make ourselves. We may not want to admit as much, but it is true. There will be times when the devil will attack you. There will be occasions when you will suffer for righteousness' sake. In most cases, though, the trouble you encounter will be a result of mistakes you make. Repent of them, learn from them and go on.

One afternoon I threw an empty tuna fish can in the trash. Later that evening, I pushed the trash down in an effort to tie the bag and take it out to the trash can. As I did, my thumb encountered the sharp lid of the can that had somehow remained upright in the trash. Its edge cut me all the way to the bone. I couldn't get the gash to stop bleeding and had to use my other hand to keep blood from leaking over everything I touched. My wife had to drive me to the emergency room to get it stitched shut.

Sheepdogs Among the Flock

You can imagine the expression on the emergency room doctor's face when he asked me how I cut myself. The wound took some time to heal, and it was quite a nuisance trying to button my shirts with only one usable thumb.

Surprisingly, my initial reaction was anger. I was mad that I had done something that could have been so easily avoided that resulted in pain and loss. I had to repent of being dumb enough to throw away a sharp object in such a careless manner, and then repent for getting angry about it. It wasn't a sign from God or an attack of the adversary. I calmed down after a while and talked to God about the situation, and He talked to me.

Did I learn anything from this ordeal? You bet I did. Now, I put every can lid inside the can and squeeze the can shut so that can never happen again. It made such an impression on some of my family members that they do the same thing. It wasn't until years later that we obtained one of those nifty can openers that leave no sharp edges on the can or the lid. I don't take any chances—I still try to fit the lid inside and squeeze the can shut as well as I am able.

A quote often misattributed to a world-famous actor says, "Life is hard; it's even harder when you're stupid."[13] I might add that it's harder yet when something bad happens because you are stupid, and you try to blame it on someone or something else.

Adversity that comes as a result of our own mistakes and wrong choices can be dealt with in a relatively straightforward manner. We should repent, ask forgiveness of God and man and go on from there. That is not too difficult to understand. It is when we have been doing things right and trouble comes that we have difficulty determining why.

SOMETIMES OTHER PEOPLE CAUSE PROBLEMS FOR US

When those who call themselves our enemies criticize us, it doesn't take us by surprise—that's what opponents do. We tend to be on guard about these kinds of threats. We certainly must be sober and vigilant, because our adversary walks about as a roaring lion, seeking whom he may devour. The devil's purpose is to steal from you, kill you, or destroy you any way he can, and if he can use a known enemy, so much the better. But the devil is also a deceiver and will try to lull you into a sense of false security regarding people who may be close to you.

The threats that are most dangerous are not from the person down the street who hurls epithets at you when he drives past your church building. The person you really need to watch out for is the one who smiles in your face while looking for a place to stick the knife in your back. The devil doesn't fight fair, and he will look for any advantage he can use to attack you.

David said in Psalm 55:12-14:

For it is not an enemy who reproaches me; then I could bear it. Nor is it one who hates me who has exalted himself against me; then I could hide from him. But it was you,

*my peer, my guide, and my acquaintance. We took pleas-
ant counsel together, and walked to the house of God in
company.*

It is particularly disappointing when someone you work
with or work for becomes an adversary. Bickering, betrayal
and strife between coworkers in the kingdom of God causes
us to appear no different than the world, and it should never
happen in gospel ministry. I have heard horror stories about
schemes that would make Mephistopheles (in literature, an
agent of the devil) look like a rookie when it came to plotting and executing plans to discredit and destroy good-
hearted helpers who found themselves, through no fault of
their own, on the wrong side of the wrong people.

What should you do when someone is trying to under-
mine your authority, destabilize your work environment, or
in some cases work behind the scenes to get you fired? Your
best recourse in such instances is to take the matter to immediate and fervent prayer. There are times when you may
be able to communicate effectively enough to resolve a conflict with such an intractable foe, but if they were reasonable, they would not have escalated things to such a state in
the first place. Only in extreme or longstanding circumstances should you make the matter known to your shepherd.

There was one occasion when someone in a position of
authority for a season tried to maneuver me into a position
where my credibility, effectiveness and job would have
come to a sudden and inglorious end. I did not know the

extent of the mischief, nor did I know that I was one of the people on his hit list. I was shocked to discover that such machinations could happen among God's people.

I do know that as I prayed with increasing urgency about the situation, God spoke to my wife in a dream and gave us wisdom to know exactly what to do. A short while later, the issue was resolved, and the troublemaker was gone.

One of the things I appreciate most about my colleagues at World Harvest Church is that none of them are striving for position or prestige. They don't get upset about who preaches, or who gets to go to certain events, or who does what, and when and how much. There were some over the years who had that attitude, but they didn't stay very long.

If you are a sheepdog in a larger flock, you must learn how to get along not only with the shepherd and the sheep, but also with the other sheepdogs. Ministry involves subordinating what you want to what God wants.

The love of God rejoices in the success of others, not just in meeting personal goals. Be thankful when someone else gets the chance to do whatever you would like to do. God knows what He has called you to, and He will not let your gifts lie dormant forever. Your celebration of someone else's success may be the key that releases you into an aspect of ministry God has for you.

What If You Feel Like
You Should Leave Your Position?

If events have occurred that cause you to wonder about whether you should stay where you are, there is an extremely important factor to consider before making any kind of change.

Did God speak to you about where you are now? If you have been there for any length of time, He probably did. Did God change His mind? Romans 11:29 says God does not change when it comes to the distribution of His gifts and callings. I believe *where* you fulfill His will is just as vital as *what* you do and *when* you do it. God is not capricious and does not make us guess about His will. I am convinced He does not authorize people to bounce around from church to church like so many pinballs, either.

If God hasn't given you additional direction, stay where you are. You don't have to wonder if you are in the will of God as long as you are doing the last thing He told you. You always need to be open to the Lord for whatever direction He gives you, but don't become concerned if you haven't heard anything specific about a change in your future. Just keep doing what you have the opportunity to do and do it with all your heart as unto the Lord.

Every year when our Bible college students graduate, I hear about the plans they have and the doors that are opening for them, and I can't help being tempted to become envious. Their lives are in front of them, filled with possibilities. I know I will be staying at the church, doing my best to provide an example for another group who will arrive in a few months. The graduates will see things I will never see and do things I will never do. I rejoice at their successes, and weep at their difficulties, but I know my place is at the church.

I feel like David waiting at the gate of the city to hear a report of how the battle is going. I am confident of victory, but wish I could be in the field with the troops. However, I must not let the reports of either conquests or disasters on the battlefield cause me to abandon my post. Only when all of us work together in the body of Christ will we see the victories God desires for us. So, every year I stay, and every year they go. Each of us will be rewarded for doing our part.

If you leave your position of opportunity too soon, God may require you to go back and do it over—correctly. College students who withdraw from a class that is already in session can't just go back to the same class the next year and start again in whatever week they quit the year before. They have to register, pay tuition and take the entire course over again. When you return, whether to a job, a college course or whatever you have left undone, the attitude you take back with you will no doubt be quite different than the one you had when you left. This is part of the growth process God is trying to work out in you.

At other times, you may have to return to the place where you stopped obeying God so your power to function can be restored. 2 Kings 6:1-7 tells of how Elisha and the sons of the prophets went to an area near the Jordan River to build a larger place for them to dwell. One student was cutting down a tree when his axe head flew off and fell in the river. This was a great loss, because not only could he no longer work, but he had no way of repaying the owner for the lost axe. Elisha asked him where the axe head came off. The young man showed him, and the prophet made the iron float to the surface and swim back to shore so it could be recovered.

When you lose your ability to fulfill your purpose, you need to be honest about what happened. Only after you take a straightforward moral inventory and acknowledge your loss will God grant you the ability to recover your strength and start over again. He will often make you go back to where you lost it and recover it there, since it's most likely to be found exactly where it fell. It would be useless to try to recover something where it has never been.

If we offend a brother or a sister, we are supposed to go to them and seek reconciliation. If we have stolen something, we need to restore it. If we have bitterness and resentment in our hearts, we must forgive before we can move forward. These are fundamental principles that have often been overlooked as causes for the lack of power in the body of Christ.

Yes, you can go back home again, but it will be more difficult if you left with a bad attitude, a critical spirit or without giving proper notice of your intentions. Your departure should not happen under a cloud of controversy. Do your part to maintain a good relationship with those who loved you, received you and gave you an opportunity to serve—don't burn your bridges behind you.

The prodigal son's situation is an example of the kind of difficulty people face when leaving improperly. He went through some hardships before he came to himself and went back home. When he arrived there, his father received him, but his elder brother rejected and ridiculed him. The prodigal didn't let that keep him from returning. Even though he had to work *with* his brother, he didn't work *for* him. When he left home, the younger brother's purpose was to please himself. When he came back, his purpose was the same as yours—to please the Father.

DON'T BE MOVED

There are two things that must not move you as a faithful sheepdog: people's praise or criticism. If you want to get an idea of how you are doing, take a tip from statisticians. When they are figuring averages, they will not include the highest and the lowest figures in their calculations, because they are known as outliers. In the same way, we should not always think that what our biggest supporters or our fiercest critics say is the last word, since the truth is likely to be somewhere between those two extremes.

Recognize that even though you will not get all the credit you deserve, neither will you get all the criticism you deserve. These things tend to balance out over time. It is more important to know that God approves of your efforts than it is to have the praise of men. In the same way, if you are conscientious at all, you are probably your own worst critic. Unless you haven't been paying attention, seldom will someone tell you about a deficiency in your performance of which you aren't already aware.

Neither praise nor criticism indicates the will of God for you, nor does it confirm whether or not you are meeting the expectations God has of you. Some people are slaves to other people's opinions. Your happiness should not depend on what other people think of you. If it does, get ready for an extremely unhappy life.

Your satisfaction as a sheepdog doesn't come from people. It doesn't even come from your shepherd, even though you certainly want him to be pleased with what you do. Your lasting satisfaction should come from knowing that God loves you and blesses your efforts in His kingdom. The acclaim of men will fade and be forgotten, but the favor of God will endure forever.

We have the wrong idea about what it means to get ahead, especially since we live in a culture saturated with shameless self-promotion. Many want their fifteen minutes of fame so desperately that they will endure any indignity to get it. No doubt fame has its rewards. It also has its penalties, but you won't find out about any of them from the celebrity tabloids.

What does it really mean to be promoted? Is it getting the big salary, or the corner office, or your name on the organization letterhead? These might be regarded as metrics of fame by the world's standards, but how do you know if you are being promoted in God's kingdom? Does promotion mean you're finally the one in charge, or that you attract the biggest crowds or have developed the largest mailing list? And if that's what promotion means, how can a humble helper ever feel eligible for it—since he may never be in front of people at all?

I propose that promotion really happens when you are better positioned to fulfill God's purposes for your life. Men may compliment you and even exalt you, but genuine promotion comes from the Lord, according to Psalm 75:6-7. Your fulfillment as a sheepdog doesn't come from how much money you make or how many people recognize your name. Your sense of satisfaction is highest when you are certain you are accomplishing His will. Anything that moves you closer to that goal is promotion, regardless of how many people you serve or what kind of material possessions you have.

It is never wrong to strive to become the absolute best you can be, and never right to work hard at remaining in the mudflats of mediocrity. But there is a principle that will help you make the distinction between worldly striving and godly contentment—and it has nothing to do with the size of the crowds or the paycheck.

We must make sure that what we are doing is God-ordained and not just a matter of fulfilling a personal ambition or goal separate from His will. When Jesus was facing the greatest crisis of His life, He prayed that the will of His Father would be done, not His. The surest way to have your dreams come to fruition is to make sure you are doing all you can to see His dream come to pass.

There has perhaps never been a harder worker in the long history of the church than the apostle Paul. He labored more rigorously than his peers, endured more ridicule and rejection than anyone other than Jesus, and had more results than those in any age since. He once had the approbation and acclaim of men, and he cast it all aside to follow Jesus to the ends of the earth.

Here's what Paul said in Philippians 4:11-13:

> ... for I have learned in whatever state I am to be content. I know both how to face humble circumstances and how to have abundance. Everywhere and in all things I have learned the secret, both to be full and to be hungry, both to abound and to suffer need. I can do all things because of Christ who strengthens me.

What I hear in these words is the testimony of a man who was seeking a reward that went far beyond the fame and fortune this world had to offer. He recognized that the riches of heaven were worth more than a worldly salary. He was satisfied with knowing he had a dwelling place in a heavenly city rather than a home in a terrestrial one. On days when he had no natural food, he was content with the spiritual sustenance that filled his soul. Whether he was abased or abounding, he could say with assurance, "This is my place." That was enough for Paul. How can we honestly claim that we require more?

CHAPTER 14

Connection and Correction

I overheard a dog owner describing his breed to some people who were interested in his pups. "They don't respond well to rough handling," he said. We need to have the same understanding about the people with whom we work. Some need more direction than others. Some respond to rebuke by redoubling their efforts, while some curl up in a corner after hearing criticism. Some are not individualists, but like to stay with the pack. Some do things on their own, while some are consensus builders. A wise shepherd learns the characteristics of the sheepdogs that help him and treats them accordingly.

As sheepdogs, we also need to learn our shepherd's particular style of doing things and do them that way. We need to adjust to the shepherd, instead of expecting the shepherd to change to accommodate us. Does your shepherd like to count the sheep? Get a calculator. Is he concerned about their physical health? Find a bottle of oil. Is he interested in outreach? Learn how to attract sheep. Does he emphasize maturity? Get acquainted with what makes sheep grow.

Sheepdogs Among the Flock

Nobody expects you to become your shepherd, but you should become more like him as you continue to work with him. You should be able to identify his likes and dislikes, his strengths and weaknesses, what excites him and what irritates him. As you do, you can begin to anticipate what he wants and produce that more consistently.

Proximity to your shepherd can be a very great blessing. There are other times when it can attract a lot of attention, negative as well as positive. If you are part of a ministry that is wreaking havoc in the devil's kingdom, be prepared for a certain amount of attention from the forces of darkness. This is not something of which you should ever be afraid, but if you are known in hell, you need to be aware of the strategies of the devil.

One of the reasons Paul suffered the things he did was because he caused so much trouble for Satan's kingdom. Paul's companions went through some things along with him. Silas comes to mind, singing at midnight in a Philippian jail right beside Paul. Jesus told His disciples, "If they hate me, don't be surprised if they hate you, too." (See John 15:18-19)

Not all of the attention is negative. I have had people come up to me nearly everywhere I go and exclaim, "I saw you on TV with Rod Parsley!" It still amazes me that I would even be on a television program, much less that anybody would make a point of mentioning it. Don't let this sort of thing go to your head, though—after all, it's not *your* television program. Just remember it could be you paying for the air time and production costs!

Each sheepdog is a unique individual. One of the tasks of leadership is to get all those who are helping bring the vision to pass working in the same direction. Not only do different people respond differently to different techniques, each helper must be aligned so they cooperate with each other without competition or unnecessary duplication of effort.

IT'S OKAY TO BE WHO YOU ARE

One of the things that really set me free in my efforts as a sheepdog was when I realized it was okay to be who I was without trying to be like someone else. We should attempt to internalize things about others we admire, and it is natural to want to copy things we see in others that we desire in ourselves. But when we become more interested in looking like someone else than becoming who God created us to be, we are in danger of losing our individuality and missing out on our assignment. The world says that imitation is the sincerest form of flattery, but if God wanted a duplicate, he would have cloned someone, and He hasn't ever done that.

For generations, young preachers have tried to emulate someone they admired or respected. Sometimes this goes to extremes. I remember hearing a friend describe how all the evangelists at one convention looked like the most successful evangelist in the organization. They wore suits with the same label and watches that looked alike. This went to such lengths that even their wives looked the same, wearing outfits from the same manufacturer and carrying the same kind of purse.

It took me a long time to realize that when someone gave me specific instructions, it wasn't because there was only one way to do something, or because they wanted me to become them. It was because they wanted me to be able to accomplish a task successfully with a minimum of disruption. I didn't have to copy what they said and how they did things (or how they looked) in order to do it right. I was free to be who I was while accomplishing the goal.

When I was in college, I enjoyed participating in the theater productions at our campus. For two years, I was in every show the university produced, at times in a leading role, necessitating a lot of character development on my part. I learned a lot and made a lot of friends, but I felt as though something wasn't right. It took some time to realize what was wrong. I tended to really get into my characters, and every time I would go from one play to the next, I kept certain distinctives of that character until it was time to learn a new one.

After a time, I lost sight of who I really was, and became extremely confused. It took me some time to shake off this confusion and come to the point where I was confident that the person I was represented the real me and not just some character I was portraying in a play. I had to become comfortable with myself.

Connection and Correction

Some years ago, I went to hear a minister who had been preaching for over fifty years. I watched with amazement as he conducted the service, doing very little himself except for directing traffic and adding a few anecdotes and illustrations at appropriate times. The rest of the time he sat on the platform and smiled while younger men and women, many of whom he had trained, did most of the ministry that night at his direction. I remember thinking how fulfilled he looked as a younger generation carried on under his tutelage. He was absolutely at ease, knowing he was fulfilling his role, as those around him were fulfilling theirs.

We must come to the point where we are comfortable with who we are both in life and in ministry. We must fulfill our assignments with grace, reflecting the glory of the Lord, not always second-guessing ourselves, filled with doubt about whether we are doing the right thing or doing it the right way.

KNOW YOUR SHEPHERD'S VOICE

As a sheepdog, I need to know that I am fulfilling a God-given role for the flock I am serving, under the direction of my shepherd, who is under the direction of the Great Shepherd. When I know I am where I am supposed to be, doing what I am supposed to do, I will have great confidence even in the midst of the most difficult of circumstances. I will be able to hear the voice of both the Great Shepherd and the undershepherd with clarity.

Jesus said in John 10:4:

Sheepdogs Among the Flock

When he brings out his own sheep, he goes before them.
And the sheep follow him, for they know his voice.

I never understood this until I heard it explained this way: In Israel, water was at a premium. There were a limited number of wells and water sources, and shepherds and their flocks would sometimes meet together at these watering holes with their flocks, perhaps at midday. The shepherds would talk while eating lunch, and the sheep would mingle together and rest, ruminating on the events of the morning.

When it was time to move on, the shepherds would simply stand up, shake the crumbs out of their garments and call to their sheep. The sheep that belonged to that shepherd would get up and follow him. None of the other sheep would move—in fact, they wouldn't even act like they heard the other shepherd. It was not the voice their ears were attuned to hear, so they paid no attention. They only moved when their shepherd called to them.

Just as the sheep need to learn to respond to the shepherd's voice, the sheepdogs need to as well. Sometimes the shepherd will need to give instruction to the sheepdogs in addition to the sheep, and if the helpers can't hear or aren't in tune, the flock may go the wrong way and wind up at the wrong destination.

What the shepherd has to say to you as a faithful sheepdog won't always be what you want to hear. Guidance and correction are necessary for all of us, sheep and sheepdogs alike. It should never be a problem for you to receive correction from those in leadership over you—that is part of their responsibility to you. None of us are without fault, and a loving overseer will help us to make necessary adjustments.

God corrects his children. I brought correction to mine—repeatedly. The reason I did is not because I didn't love them, but because I did. I knew that if I corrected them when they were small, I would have some measure of confidence that they would be self-correcting when they grew up. (They were, and they are.) However, I never corrected my neighbor's children—they weren't my responsibility.

If you never receive God's correction, you may want to check to see if you are in His family—or at least in the right household. Hebrews 12:11 says correction is never pleasant when it happens, but afterward it produces the peaceable fruit of righteousness, which should always be the goal of redemptive guidance.

1 Peter 2:5 says that we are not dead bricks, but living stones. Bricks are all the same, and one can be interchanged for pretty much any other one and put anywhere in the building. Stones are a different matter. No two are alike, and they have to be selected and placed with care so that they join with one another to build something useful. At times, stones will need to be adjusted to make sure they fit in the place the stonemason wants them. This will inevitably involve some parts of the stone being chipped away so each one will interlock with the ones around it.

Sheepdogs Among the Flock

We don't get to pick and choose where we want to serve—we get placed there by someone whose plan we may not understand and of which we may not even be aware. But wherever we are placed, our purpose is to do our part in holding up the building.

For those who want to keep all their sharp edges, keep in mind what Jesus said in John 15:1-8 about the vine and the branches. He told His disciples that every branch that bore fruit could expect to be purged or pruned. Pruning involves cutting away what is dead, unnecessary or unfruitful so that more fruit can be produced. Fruit growers the world over follow this principle. It was God's idea first.

Much of this pruning will come as a result of communication between a pastor and those helping him. Communication is vital to every human relationship, and it is certainly a key to the interactions between leaders and their helpers. But communicating effectively seems to be an ethereal and unreachable goal for many people.

Communication is a process, not a one-time incident. It is also a complex process, involving many elements that all have an effect on the outcome. We think we know how to communicate—we have learned how to use words, gestures and expressions to make ourselves understood. But in a working relationship, there are some things that tend to short-circuit effective communication.

Connection and Correction

ASSUMPTION

Assumption is the lazy man's substitute for effective communication. It must be popular, because it happens quite often. It's better to make sure understanding is complete than to assume it is and be disappointed. There are a number of reasons assumption happens so frequently.

Someone who has a certain amount of knowledge about a situation or issue may not realize that everyone doesn't know what they know. Consequently, they may not explain what they want as carefully as they should. Or, they may say what they want, but not give specific directions about how it should be done, thinking that anyone else would do it the same way they would. When it doesn't get done, or is not done in a prescribed way, expectations are not realized and trouble results.

If directions are unclear and subordinates don't understand them, why wouldn't they ask for clarification? It's simple, really. Just think about chemistry class in high school. Nobody wanted to prolong the agony by asking a question—everyone wanted to get class over with as quickly as possible. But the real reason nobody asked a question about the carbon dating process or how to make oxygen was because nobody wanted to be thought of as stupid or lacking understanding.

The same kind of thing happens in ministry. A helper may not ask because he doesn't want to be regarded as anything other than sharp, astute, erudite, smart or any of a

193

thousand other adjectives. But if you don't solve an ignorance problem sooner, it will show up later—when the directive is undone, or the project is either unfulfilled or just plain wrong. If you're going to fail, do it at the beginning, not at the end. Success at last will overcome failure at first.

Here's another important point about assumption: don't assume you have communicated just because you left a message, fired off an email or sent a text. The world of electronic commerce is filled with trolls, demons, sprites, haunts, boogers and other plagues too numerous to name, and they never sleep. They will be more than happy to purloin your carefully constructed attempt at communication to assure it will never make it to its assigned destination. A telltale sign of assumption is the indignant cry: "But I sent you an email!"

Here's the antidote: always ask for a reply. If you don't get one, you almost certainly haven't communicated, since feedback closes the communication loop. If you do get a reply, you may have communicated, but even then, it's not guaranteed. Communication also involves the receiver understanding your message, not just receiving it.

While you're waiting for feedback from others, don't neglect to send it to those who have sent you messages. Prompt, clear, and concise responses are always appreciated by those for whom you work and those with whom you interact, whether they tell you so or not.

NONVERBAL CUES ARE POWERFUL

We tend to think that words are the most important part of any communication interaction. The words we choose certainly have an impact. Some words are more helpful than others—and some are more harmful. Kids on the playground used to say, "Sticks and stones may break my bones, but words will never harm me." That's just not true. Sticks and stones may break my bones, but words will break my heart. Be careful how you choose and use your words. Keep them sweet—you never know when you will have to eat them.

Even more important than the words we use are the non-verbal cues that go with them. Effective communicators know that their interactions will be more powerful when their words, gestures, expressions and inflections align with one another. In fact, researchers have found that when words and nonverbal cues are in conflict, people tend to believe what they see and how they feel instead of the words they hear. If I frown at you when I tell you I love you, I am sending you a mixed message, and one that is likely to be misunderstood, or even disbelieved. Here's one way to remember this truth: people will probably not remember exactly what you say—but they will always remember how you made them feel.

FAILING TO LISTEN

Another thing that can disrupt communication is failure to listen. Listening is a lost art in our culture. Part of the problem is there are more messages than ever before, and they all clamor for our attention. Serenity is an unknown quantity in much of the world. People today seem to need noise. Solitude is regarded as the esoteric pursuit of a few ascetics who are regarded as curiosities. Most people get nervous if there is no sound for sixty seconds—even in, or I might say, *especially* in church services.

Patient listening is a necessary skill for all ministry helpers to develop. It is important not only for ministry to those under your care, but in your interactions with those over you. Failure to listen not only compromises your effectiveness in following directions, but indicates a lack of respect for those who deserve your respect and whose goodwill you need.

Here's a principle to keep in mind when around those who are over you in the Lord: you already know what you know. What you don't know and need to learn is probably locked up in someone else's heart or mind. Your access to it depends on the measure of respect you give to them—and one important way to tell them you respect them is to listen to them. Be quiet, and let others speak.

Do more than just hear the words they say—listen for the meaning between or even behind the words. If or when you have the chance to respond, ask more questions instead of offering more opinions. By doing these things, you may not become one of the wisest counselors, but at least your leaders won't mind when you have a seat at the table.

Connection and Correction

Shepherds around the world have depended on their faithful sheepdogs to help them with many necessary tasks in caring for the sheep. It's always been a pleasure for me to watch a well-trained working dog interacting with an owner or handler who knows it well and understands it. It is a beautiful thing.

Sometimes the shepherd will give commands to the dog by hand and sometimes by voice. Then there are times when it seems like the dog knows what its owner wants without any direction at all. This may seem like a mystery, but it is actually the result of a long and fruitful relationship between them.

As a faithful ministry helper, you can develop this same kind of insight into what your leader wants. It doesn't come overnight, and there is a lot of learning that needs to be done, but it can be accomplished.

CHAPTER 15

Entering and Leaving

My father was always perturbed by people who threw trash on the ground. He was continually picking up things other people left behind and disposing of them properly. It was bad enough when someone accidentally littered, but even worse when they did it intentionally. He was a firm believer that you should not leave a mess for someone else to clean up.

The same thing is true for sheepdogs. Don't leave a situation in worse shape than it was when you came on the scene, because someone will have to pick up after you when you leave. Unresolved issues left behind never unravel themselves, but always require someone else to invest time and effort to fix them. You need to deal with the situations that occur on your watch, and not just leave them for the next person to try to decipher.

LEAVE THINGS BETTER THAN YOU FOUND THEM

Even when unfinished business is unavoidable, it can cause problems. Years ago, I had a loan with a bank. After the loan had been paid off, I kept receiving statements from the bank showing that I had a zero balance. I didn't think any more about it. About ten months later, I heard from someone at the bank who assured me our account was now being closed. I told him I thought it had been closed long ago.

It seems the bank employee who was in charge of my account had taken an extended leave of absence due to illness, and then died. It took some time for the bank to assign another employee to the accounts he left behind, and even more time to figure out all the details of the accounts that had been in limbo all that time.

Don't leave loose ends. Make sure things are tied up and in proper order before you leave a ministry position. Those who follow you shouldn't have to take six months to rectify problems you left behind.

One of the fundamentals of principled camping is to always leave a campsite in better condition than you found it. This ought to be adopted by sheepdogs everywhere. If you leave the fold, that flock should be in better condition when you leave than they were when you came.

This deserves emphasis, because how you leave one situation or job is how you will enter the next one. If you left your last place of employment to try to avoid conflict, you will be likely to run away the first time conflict occurs at your new place of employment. If your attitude needed adjustment on the last job, it will surely need it on the next one. If you couldn't follow the rules at the old place, you won't follow them at the new place.

People seldom leave their baggage behind—they tend to bring it with them. Don't start a new position or assume new responsibilities with the disadvantage of unresolved conflicts that are sure to hunt you down and disable you.

You're not ready to move forward unless you're sure everything is good at your last place of employment, or as good as you can make it. If you are sure you have done that, here are some recommendations that will help you get a good start wherever you're going.

KNOW WHAT YOU'RE GETTING INTO

It is essential to get an agreement in writing when dealing with employment issues. A verbal agreement or a brief conversation of a general nature is insufficient. This is an issue that involves your effectiveness as well as your protection. You cannot fulfill expectations in a work environment if you don't know what those expectations are, and you won't be able to remember specifics unless they are written down. Don't assume anything about what you are supposed to be doing, or how, or when.

A colleague of mine moved on to work for another ministry during a time of transition for that ministry. He began his new job without any specific duties, hours or even a rudimentary job description. All he had was a vague commitment from his employer to get together and talk about it at an indefinite time.

Sheepdogs Among the Flock

Needless to say, when a commitment for employment was finally made, it was far different from the understanding he had when he came to town. The amount of money he would actually be paid was about one-third less than the amount that was mentioned to him in his initial conversation. He was unable to stay there and had to move on. All this could have been avoided if he had insisted on a written employment agreement.

Make sure you have your shepherd's understanding about what you will be doing. Some shepherds give general directions and expect you, as a faithful and sensible sheepdog, to have enough sense to figure out what to do. Other shepherds have a very keenly developed sense of how they want things accomplished, and to do it another way, even if it gets the correct result, is unacceptable. Some shepherds are more interested in the process, and others are only interested in the end result. Neither one is wrong, but as a sheepdog working with the flock under their supervision, you need to find out not only *what* needs done, but *how* it needs to be done.

If there are responsibilities and expectations about your new position that are not clear, get them resolved immediately. When in doubt, ask the right questions of the right people, and do it sooner rather than later. A clear understanding beforehand will keep you from having a misunderstanding afterward. Don't be afraid to ask questions, and take every chance you can to watch and learn from others you see doing the same sorts of things you will be doing.

Entering and Leaving

As a new helper, whether you are an employee or a volunteer, you will sometimes encounter mistrust and suspicion from those already there. On the other hand, you may feel like the new kid in the third-grade class at school, and that can keep you from trusting and reaching out to those who can help you the most. In either case, these problems can be avoided.

When new people join a local church, or become part of a leadership effort, there are equal parts of reservations and free passes given by the congregation. Reservations happen because the new person is inevitably different from the previous one, and he will do things differently and will think differently from those who did the same tasks in the past. Most people are naturally resistant to change and the uncertainty that it brings.

However, there is a measure of grace often extended to someone just starting out with a new church, or someone who has new responsibilities within an existing church. This honeymoon period is necessary to allow a new person to become adjusted to a new environment and new ways of doing things.

New people can minimize the reservations people have about them by refusing to criticize former leaders or individuals in positions of responsibility and by developing relationships with those in their new surroundings before creating too much change.

Sheepdogs Among the Flock

RESPECT THE EXISTING CULTURE

It is important that a newcomer respect the traditions and culture that have already been developed in a work or fellowship setting. Anyone who comes in with an attitude that they know better than anyone else will have a hard time becoming accepted among those who have endured a few hard knocks along the way to get where they are now.

The old oak tree stood in the middle of the forest, the greatest among the trees. It had been there for over a hundred years and was more than a hundred feet tall. One fine spring day, a vine sprouted up next to the oak tree and rapidly climbed up its trunk. Finally, at the end of the summer, the vine emerged above the branches at the crown of the old oak. Feeling very cocky at its ascent in such an abbreviated time, it began to taunt the oak tree.

"How long have you been standing here?" the vine said.

"About a hundred years," the oak tree replied.

"And how tall are you?" the vine said.

"About a hundred feet tall," the oak tree said.

"You mean it took you a hundred years to grow a hundred feet? I have grown taller than you, and it took me just a couple of months. Look at me! Look at me, everybody! I'm taller than the oak tree!"

The vine tormented the oak tree every day for weeks. Then one clear night the first frost came, and the vine withered and fell to the ground, dead.

The oak tree sighed. "They say that every year," it said.

Entering and Leaving

I remember one occasion when a new administrator was brought on to help with the multiplying job duties that came with a rapidly-growing ministry. Within a short time, we had moved just about every employee and every piece of furniture in the offices to increase efficiency. A few days later, we rearranged everything into a different configuration, moving everyone into different offices again. We did become more efficient at moving, but it didn't help endear our new administrator to the staff.

The old hands can help the acclimation process for new people, however. Instead of standing off and taking bets on how long a newbie will last, veterans can jump in and help out by answering questions and offering their assistance. I have helped people move in, taken them to dinner, pointed out where things were in their new community, gone over policies and procedures, toured the facilities with them and generally tried to be helpful. Sometimes they stayed and sometimes they didn't.

New people in a church or old people with new responsibilities can be quite good for a body of believers. The last seven words of a dying church are, "We've never done it that way before." When we have done things often enough that they become routine, we fail to see approaches or insights that keep us from becoming stale. I can proofread a document a dozen times and miss something that another person will spot right away. New eyes see new things, and sometimes the new things are just the things that will keep you on track or lead you to new victories.

Sheepdogs Among the Flock

KEEP YOUR DEPARTURE PROFESSIONAL

A question that inevitably comes up with sheepdogs employed by churches is how to go about leaving if and when the time comes. I always encourage people to get input from the shepherd about such a move first, rather than last. This is not only proper naturally, but is in accordance with spiritual order. How would you feel as a shepherd when those around you who have been entrusted to take care of the sheep just leave without any advance notice, or very little notice? The sheep are upset, the shepherd is upset, and everyone is at a disadvantage.

Working in a position of trust with God's people is not like working at a factory or retail store. A church may be regarded as a business, but it is a people business that is based on relationships, not on manufacturing a product or selling a service. A two-week notice may be sufficient at a fast-food restaurant, but not in the house of God.

Too often, those with a responsibility to the sheep don't fulfill their duty to leave the sheepfold in the proper manner. I have often seen people make their plans, then ask the shepherd to bless them as they go. Their departure leaves a gap that other people have to fill, which is problematic when no one has yet been raised up to take their place. Sometimes it takes a department or an area of ministry years to recover from a sudden resignation. It takes time to train people who are new to certain tasks, and it also takes time for them to develop the same trust and leadership skills previous leaders may have had.

Again, put yourself in the shepherd's place. You have been doing whatever you have done for years. Now you want to leave, and you give little advance notice. You say that it is God moving you on. Unless you are an unusually capricious person, you won't make this decision without giving it a considerable amount of thought, more often than not over a long period of time. Now you have your mind made up, but your pastor is at a great disadvantage, because he hasn't been part of the process.

How is your pastor supposed to respond to this? Should he try to persuade you to stay, knowing that your heart has already departed, and you will not be able to do your work willingly any longer? Is he supposed to bless you as you go, knowing that he will have hurting people who will require an explanation of your departure, and knowing that he will also have to find another person to take your place? It is a no-win proposition for the shepherd, and one they face time after time because of the short-sightedness and self-centeredness of their helpers.

There are times when family emergencies or other extreme situations demand immediate action, and changes have to be made on the spur of the moment. But far more often, I have seen exits that have been made with little or no thought given to the well-being of either the pastor or the congregation he leads. Sometimes these departures happen in the middle of the night, with no notice at all. How do you explain a situation like that to a church in a way that sounds sensible? You can't, because it makes no sense, and should never happen in the body of Christ. If you accept a position of responsibility over the flock of God, you should be willing and prepared to see it through to a proper conclusion.

HOW DO YOU LEAVE A MINISTRY POSITION?

What is the proper procedure for leaving?

The first and underlying principle is to speak to your pastor about your inclination to move on—far ahead of time. Nobody should know about it before he does, except your spouse if you are married. This will give you and your pastor the chance to discuss the options and the timing that will create the least disturbance.

Once you have spoken to the pastor, you are not automatically at liberty to discuss your decision with anyone else. The timing of who knows about your departure may need to be carefully managed, and you need to follow this rule: if anyone knows, everyone knows. Don't say anything to anyone without permission, because regardless of how discreet they may seem, people you trust may not be able to remain silent about it. Colleagues, volunteers and church members will become uneasy if they hear things from the gospel grapevine instead of from their leadership.

Keep your head down and your guard up during the time between your discussion with your pastor and the time of your departure or its announcement. You may hear from people in a roundabout way who will try to sound you out about your intentions. They may have suspicions because your pastor may have had to consult others to get a better idea of what decisions to make in light of your impending departure, and those people, although told in confidence, may not be as trustworthy as they appear.

Don't yield to the temptation to slack off in your work just because your time there is ending. The work of the kingdom still goes on, and people have needs that don't stop just because you are leaving.

Whether or not an announcement will be made to the church as a whole is dependent on many factors, and a final decision should be made by the pastor, not by you. If you are a long-term employee and you have to leave because of a family situation or other problem that is easily explained, it's more likely that an announcement will be made in a service. If the circumstances are less than favorable and easily misconstrued, don't be surprised if your departure is not mentioned.

If your leaving is not on good terms, it will mean that the relationships you have made with the people you have served will of necessity come to an end. They will not be joining you in your new endeavor, and their lives will go on without you. Don't expect them to be your best friends on social media. Move on, and don't do anything to disturb their tranquility. Neither farewell dinners nor long tearful goodbyes will be helpful to you or to them.

Sometimes people will want to follow you when you leave. Unless you have a formal arrangement with your pastor for this to happen, you should never allow this to occur. You said God spoke to you to leave, but your word is not their word. Tell anyone who plans to leave the church with you or after you to stay right where they are, and tell them in no uncertain terms. Then tell your pastor who they are. Otherwise, you might be guilty of troubling someone else's flock. Keep in mind the Old Testament penalty for sheep-stealing was fourfold restoration.

The principle of sowing and reaping applies to areas other than money. If you leave peacefully and sow seeds of peace, you will enter your next opportunity in peace and reap its harvest. If you sow strife and discord, you will reap the fruit of that unholy harvest. And this applies to you after you leave, as well as while you are leaving. Your departure does not give you liberty to soil and smear the reputation of those for whom you worked.

A well-known evangelist came to our church and talked about his relationship with his mentor, who died many years before under questionable circumstances. Rumors of his mentor's alleged dissolute lifestyle had circulated among believers for decades. "Everything I know about him is good," the evangelist said. He would know better than most, since he worked under the man for years. There is an old saying: "If you can't say anything good, don't say anything at all." It's still good advice.

What Happens When Church Members Leave?

What about when church members leave? Obviously, people and congregations will change as they move through time. Some folks will come and remain in one place for years—even decades. But in our highly mobile culture, it is likely that many people will come and go. There are lots of reasons this may happen. There is a way departures can be handled that maximize goodwill and minimize disruption for the individuals and the church.

Those who leave in peace are the easy cases. Perhaps the most common reasons folks move on is due to a change in their job or family situation. It's not hard to see how someone needs to move if they can't find a job in their field in the city or community where they currently live. In addition, more and more people are finding it necessary to provide care to a family member and need to relocate to do so. Some will get married or move away to fulfill their life's dreams elsewhere. Others need to move for educational opportunities or because of military service.

If they have been in any form of leadership, even volunteer leadership, it is never appropriate for them to leave without making those over them aware of the change that they are contemplating. This is because arrangements need to be made for a smooth transition when someone else assumes their responsibilities. This is not always possible, but it is always desirable and creates the best opportunity for satisfactory transition.

Regardless of how difficult it can be to see good people move away, we need to remember they are God's people. They will ultimately be accountable to Him for how, where and when they fulfill His purpose. There are several things you can do to bless them before they move on.

Always commit them to God's grace and care. We can be sure He will be with them if they are moving to follow God's will for their lives. Ask God to guide them to a place of fellowship with other saints where the word of God is proclaimed and believed, and where the love of God is demonstrated. I always attempt to recommend a church to them if I know of one in the area to which they are moving.

Let them know that you will always consider them to be a part of the church, whether or not their names are on the active membership roster. Thank them for their service and sacrifice over the years. After all, if they were participants in any area of the local body, their prayers, faith, service and finances helped the church become what it is. Tell them that you look forward to seeing them again. Assure them that they are welcome to return whenever they have the opportunity. Ask them to give you their new contact information, and request that they stay in touch with you so that you can continue to rejoice with them in their victories and pray with them through their challenges.

I have never been made aware of anyone who left feeling slighted or unappreciated when I took these steps with them prior to their departure.

Those who do not leave in peace are another matter altogether. Whenever and wherever humans get together, there will inevitably be misunderstanding, miscommunication, unfortunate assumptions, and hurt feelings. Sometimes these and similar issues lead to people separating from fellowship on terms that are less than peaceful and respectful. How do we handle these kinds of situations?

First and foremost, reconciliation should be sought between the offenders and those who have been offended. One of the most common reasons this does not take place is because those who are offended don't give any indication to the offender that anything is amiss until they leave the fellowship. They will be quick to rehearse the wrong with their friends and acquaintances, but those people are not the ones who can bring restoration to the matter. In addition, family and friends are most likely to be the ones who will take the part of anyone offended in any controversy.

Even if reconciliation is not possible, there should be no bitterness or resentment held toward those who have left improperly. Over the years, I have seen people who left with anger or bitterness return with a completely different attitude and become a valuable and vital part of the church. God has a way of dealing with His people wherever they are, and it is His goodness that will lead them to repentance and restoration. We can help this restoration take place by having an attitude of forgiveness and grace toward anyone who has departed, regardless of the reason.

Two characteristics of any living thing are intake and discharge. The church is a living thing, and people will come in and out regularly. When this is done with love and grace, the result will be growth, strength and continued peace even in the midst of change.

CHAPTER 16

Troublesome Sheep and How to Deal with Them

My cousin lived near a sheep barn owned by the farmer who lived down the road. The barn was old and in need of repair, and from time to time the sheep would find their way out into the surrounding barnyard at the most inconvenient times. It was uncanny how they could get out of the most inconspicuous gap between boards or through a hole in the fence. Where one went, the others would surely follow. Getting them back in was another matter. They could be the most contrary and downright stupid animals when it came to keeping them safe. They could find their way out, but they couldn't find their way back in. The more frustrated we became with them, the more frantic and disoriented their behavior.

You will find that some people can get themselves into the most convoluted and difficult messes with little or no effort, but they can't seem to find their way back out. In addition, they will resist your best efforts to help them see the way out of their dilemma. Becoming upset or impatient with them will only amplify their difficulties. They may even begin to see *you* as their problem and fail to acknowledge any personal responsibility for their situation.

Sheepdogs should by nature be patient and longsuffering. If you can't put up with a certain amount of irresponsibility, you should probably think about doing something else. But you also need to recognize the difference between mistakes people make that are due to ignorance and words or actions that are calculated to cause harm.

The Bible is full of examples of men who dealt graciously and compassionately with those who opposed them. Jesus even forgave those who crucified Him. You can bear quite a lot of opposition and still accomplish the will of God for your life. But when those for whom we lay our lives down suffer loss because of someone else's ungodly behavior, we get stirred up.

Here is the trigger that turns loose the corrective side of the sheepdog—under the shepherd's direction, of course: when an individual's actions threaten to harm other sheep. When someone puts the well-being of other sheep in jeopardy, they have to be corrected. Failure to do so is just as wrong, and perhaps even more dangerous, than being too harsh and restrictive with the offender.

When someone begins to hurt someone else in the church, disturb their peace, attempt to cause them to suffer loss or cause some other kind of trouble, we must not hide our heads in the sand and pretend it isn't happening. Problems don't go away by themselves, and usually it is not the shepherd, but the sheepdog who is delegated to deal with it.

I once heard a well-known children's minister say, "This full gospel light draws a lot of strange bugs."[14]

Ministry helpers know that's true, since we often see the less attractive aspects of the body of Christ. Whether a natural or a spiritual body, there are some things that are just supposed to remain covered. You will surely get your share of exposure to the not-so-pretty aspects of people's attitudes and behavior. There are certain categories of sheep that will bug you and cause more problems than others.

TYPES OF TROUBLESOME SHEEP

One category of troublesome sheep is what I call the **spiritually-minded ones**. To them, everything has a spiritual component, and there is a spiritual remedy for every problem. This could involve everything from the temperature of the room to why their car won't start. Their answer to everything is prayer and spiritual warfare.

These people are seldom dangerous, but they can be extremely annoying. They can also be very obstinate, especially when you won't agree with their point of view. They tend to be contrarians, and for this reason don't attract many adherents. They can also be some of the loudest responders in a service, which can cause others, especially visitors who are not used to that sort of thing, to become uncomfortable.

Unfortunately, they usually won't agree when you tell them that some problems are the result of poor decision-making or lack of good sense on their part. These folks often need repeated explanations that everything is not spiritual in nature, and that their insistence that nothing else could be wrong will only prolong their difficulties.

A similar type of person is someone *who thinks everything that happens to them is the result of demon spirits*. If you haven't encountered this type yet, you surely will.

There are two extremes when it comes to the devil. The first is to deny his existence. To discount that the devil and demonic activity is real is to ignore the testimony of Jesus and the book of Acts. The other extreme is to attribute everything bad that happens to the operation of demons. This is also a perversion of the truth. It leads to paralyzing fear and a refusal to accept responsibility for actions and decisions that may be the real reasons for whatever problems are occurring.

A lady was convinced she was tormented by demons. She complained of unending distress. I asked her what kinds of symptoms she was experiencing, and she said she could feel the demon spirits running up and down her arms and legs, because they had hot feet.

I was puzzled by this, but then had an idea I thought would help. I don't ever recommend asking a woman to reveal her age, but in some cases it is unavoidable. I asked her how old she was. She said she had just turned fifty. It may have been rather indelicate of me, but I recommended that she make an appointment with her doctor to ask about the signs of menopause and what could be done about it. She did and had no more problems with hotfooted demon spirits.

Another category is what I refer to as **roadies.** These folks are the ones who make a living traveling from place to place depending on the benevolence of churches or the good will of saints to give them handouts. Some of them are the most talented storytellers I have ever heard, but their assorted tales of woe always have similar characteristics.

They always have an emergency that is incredibly urgent—a pregnant wife, a sick baby or a death in the family. There is a specific amount of money they need immediately. They have no family or friends on whom they can depend — or with whom you can verify their story, or even their identity. They will usually promise to repay whatever they are asking you to give them. They will do their best to make you feel guilty about turning them down. They will explain their need and plead their case for as long as it takes to get what they want.

They don't want employment, a place to live or prayer. They want cash. And if you give it to them, you'll never see it again. The only thing you will have a reasonable likelihood of expecting is that the money will not be used for the purpose for which it was given.

Every church needs to develop a standard procedure for dealing with such requests, and every ministry helper should know what it is and follow it scrupulously.

And then there are *people who have a behavioral health issue*, medically diagnosed or not, that may result in unusual or even bizarre behavior. These folks need an additional measure of compassionate ministry, since they are dealing with limitations most of us will never know. They should be encouraged to participate in as much of the life of the church as they are able, but there may be occasions when their behavior is out of control. In most instances this happens because they either have no access to medication or they have not taken it as prescribed.

They need to be referred to a family member, other caregiver or a medical professional. In the event they have none, it may be necessary to assign a level-headed and firm volunteer to them when they are at church, to monitor their behavior and help them understand what is appropriate and what is not.

A lady who obviously needed ministry walked into the church one afternoon. Another young minister was available, so I thought it would be a good opportunity to help him learn how to deal with situations like these. I told him he would take the lead and I would sit in with him.

He began to ask the lady questions to try to determine how we could help her. Her answers became more and more confused and erratic. She made a remark about the Holy Spirit, and my colleague, in an effort to ascertain her spiritual condition, said, "Who is the Holy Spirit?"

"I am the Holy Spirit," she said, as soberly as a judge.

My colleague had never before encountered anything like this. I will never forget the expression on his face. He looked at me as if to say, "Okay, Mister Big Shot Senior Elder, what do we do now?"

We eventually managed to get some contact information out of her and called her family. She had gone off all her medications and had been missing for three days. They were overjoyed to know that she was safe and came to the church to get her. They were relieved—and so were we.

Yet another kind is ***people who have fixations, obsessions, paranoia or who are conspiracy theorists***. In some cases, they may also belong to the preceding category. Whether they do or not, they may benefit from a referral to a medical professional, which you should not hesitate to make if you feel it would be helpful to them.

I am in no way trying to make any kind of professional diagnosis here, but you don't have to be a professional to recognize these folks. They will not talk very long before their special issue comes up, and that is just about the only thing they will ever mention.

There is no way to predict what the issue will be or how it got started. It may be that they are convinced they have blasphemed the Holy Spirit and are beyond hope of redemption. They might be obsessed with cleanliness, and the thought of germs fills them with dread. Some people think they are being followed or watched by the authorities, or someone who means them harm. Sometimes they are sure they are supposed to marry someone who has no interest or desire in developing a relationship with them. In other cases, they have a revelation, a crusade or a cause that is so important that it demands all their time and attention. Some folks are certain they have a sure-fire cure for a medical condition or diagnosis. Others are convinced they have a calling from God to do something beyond the boundaries of Scripture or plain good sense.

There are too many categories to list them all. In the majority of these situations, the best thing you can do is try to give them calm and rational responses, without confirming or encouraging their obsessions or compulsions. This can be difficult, especially when they regard your acknowledgement of what they are saying as your approval of or agreement with whatever idea they may espouse.

Every helper needs to be sensitive to the Holy Spirit when dealing with these issues. On one hand, you don't want to demean and dismiss well-meaning people who have become entangled in error. They need gentle admonition and correction so they can recover from a wrong turn on life's highway. On the other hand, you don't want wild-eyed conspiracists who refuse correction to roam at will among the flock, causing confusion and other kinds of trouble. These people need to be lovingly but firmly confronted and warned that if they have something to say, they need to say it to you, so that you can put a stop to it before it affects others.

If it is beyond your ability to handle ministering to these people, ask for help from someone who has had more experience. In a few cases, you may be dealing with demonic oppression, and in far fewer, even possession. In these instances, especially, you should never minister to someone by yourself. When in doubt, get a second opinion, and always make the shepherd aware of what kinds of issues may threaten the well-being of the flock.

People with control issues will be a problem at times. This need or desire to control manifests itself in many different forms. One of the most frequent is the person who demands to talk to the pastor. They can't talk to anyone else, because what they have to share is too personal, too urgent, or has earth-shattering implications that could not be comprehended by others.

A man demanded to talk to the pastor just before a service began. He had never been to the church before and had no previous connection to the ministry. When he was politely denied access, he said he wanted to make a large contribution to the ministry. We told him if he wanted to make a contribution, we would provide him with an offering envelope, but he would still not be able to talk to the pastor, since the service was about to begin. He refused to talk to anyone else, and he left indignant that he couldn't just walk in and do what he wanted. Coincidentally, he had a large food stain on his tie, which didn't help his credibility.

A lady with a large feather in her hat came into the service half an hour after it began. She told everyone who would listen that she was a prophetess with a word from God for the church. She was shown a seat, which was in the back of the building, since it was packed with people. Sure enough, during the service she stood up and began to share her word aloud, which she said was from the Lord. If I remember correctly, the ushers carried her out while she was still talking.

We found out later that she was late because she got lost on the way to the church. One of our members happened to be scheduled to work that day at a convenience store where she stopped to ask directions, and we knew from his description of her that it was the same person. You would think that someone who had a special message from God would also know how to get to where the message was supposed to be delivered.

I'm not despising prophecy, but Paul gives very specific instructions about the use of the vocal gifts of the Spirit in public assemblies in 1 Corinthians 14. God doesn't interrupt Himself with those who do not submit themselves to proper authority and whose spirits are not under control.

Nearly every week, someone comes to the church with a message for Pastor Parsley. We have a procedure in place to handle requests like this. We always ask them to write down what they want to say to him, and make sure they include their contact information. They can give it to me, or to any one of the leaders, before or after a service, through the mail or online. Most of the time, they will comply.

If they want personal ministry from the pastor, I tell them that in the event no opportunity for ministry happens during the service, the elders will pray for them at the end of the service in the altar area. I seldom tell the pastor about their request, but time after time, he will minister to them without knowing that they are there with a specific need, or what their need is. It doesn't happen every time, but I have been amazed at how often it does. If it doesn't, the elders will pray for them afterward. This suffices in the majority of situations.

Every local church will do things differently, and your church will want to develop a standard model to use in these cases.

There are also ***those who use threats*** in an attempt to get what they want. You can recognize them because they always include the words *if* and *then* in their proposals. If you don't do what they want, then they will do something to cause trouble. If you don't let them talk to the pastor, then they will go the media. If you don't give them the money to pay three months' rent, then their children will be homeless. If you don't promote their pet project, then they're going to leave the church. There are a thousand other variations, but I think you can recognize this tactic.

Sheepdogs Among the Flock

This is nothing more than a form of blackmail. Don't negotiate with these people. Let them blow and bluster, and make whatever threats they want to make—to you, that is—not to others in the congregation. Then simply, politely and firmly tell them no. And after you do, tell them in no uncertain terms that this is the only time you will have this discussion with them, and you don't ever expect to hear anything about it again. This will result in one of two things happening: either they will leave and cause problems for someone else, or they will repent. I wish I could tell you that the second outcome is more likely than the first, but experience shows otherwise, by about a twenty to one ratio.

You will encounter *those who will do anything to get in front of people or be in charge.* They have to be seen and heard. They must make the decisions. They can't just be on the committee, they have to be the chairperson of the committee. They aren't satisfied being in the choir, they have to be the song leader. They won't stop at being allowed to make announcements, they will plague you for a chance to preach. They're driven to need the attention and acclaim and adoration they think being the first and the best and in the front will bring.

The best advice I can give you about this type of person is to keep them as far away from any position of authority as you can until the need to be noticed is worked out of them. Sometimes this will happen. More often they will take their leave of your church if they see their big break is not going to happen there. Bless them in their going.

False accusations and those who dare to make them are another category of problem altogether. The best way to defend against a lie is to walk in the truth in every area of your life. I've never worried much about lies circulated about my colleagues or me. The light of truth will always dispel the darkness of deception. Of course, we should warn people about the dangers of starting rumors or even listening to rumors, gossip and innuendo. They need to refuse to hear those kinds of reports and rebuke those who repeat them. Rumors and whispering campaigns can do irreparable harm to everyone who is touched by them.

Matthew 18:15-17 gives specific instructions about what believers should do if they have a controversy with one another. The first step in this process is for the offended person to go to the offender alone to discuss the matter. Much of the time, the reason gossip gets started is because people refuse to obey the clear directions of Scripture in this matter.

Instead of listening to someone talk about what "he or she said," I recommend that you get that person and the "he or she" in question together and tell them to resolve it. If they refuse, tell them in no uncertain terms that gossip is sin, and sin has serious consequences. Long tongues combined with short fuses can make big problems out of little problems. Don't tolerate talebearing.

Let's not forget *those who see a church service as an opportunity to grow their business.* Some people consider church services as a gathering of a potential customer base or a chance to promote their products or services.

Sheepdogs Among the Flock

If you want to have a church directory or a bulletin board where your members can advertise, by all means do so. In my experience, though, this will cause more problems than it will solve. Criteria must be established about who will be included, and someone will have to keep the information updated. Then there will be the problems that arise when one church member has a controversy with a brother or sister who has provided goods or services that did not meet their approval. What would have been a disagreement between two people now involves the church, since that is where the information was found. That is a burden that you don't need and don't want—but you're welcome to try it.

A bigger problem is when people try to recruit other church members for their pyramid scheme or marketing program, or who use the church parking lot to sell their wares or advertise their programs by putting flyers under the windshield wipers of automobiles. Please take my advice and don't ever allow that sort of thing to take place. People don't (or shouldn't) come to church to do their shopping or to be solicited by those who are hawking the latest fads that are making their way through the body of Christ.

You will almost certainly encounter **con men** who will call you with this line, or something like it: "I've got something to show you that will be worth a lot of money to the ministry…" I've listened to enough of these presentations to know they are not worth your time. If they are unable or unwilling to explain in a few sentences on the phone what they are talking about, you should never agree to sit down with them. If you do, you will both be disappointed in the outcome.

Decades ago, one of the scams that was in vogue was what I call a dirt pile scheme. Someone would come through town selling shares in a gold mine somewhere out West that had shut down years before. The pitch went sort of like this, as I recall: since the price of gold had increased so dramatically, it was now profitable to process gold in amounts that would not have been feasible before. Big returns could be realized on a relatively small investment. I'm sure your pastor would not want his people to pass up such a lucrative opportunity, and I'm offering it to you and your church because we got your name from a friend of yours, (insert friend's name here).

They will wrap up their presentation by telling you all the people whose names you recognize who have already signed up and ask you to put your name on their list and your money in their pocket. Wouldn't you like to see the tithes and offerings that would result from this profitable enterprise? If you're not careful, they will give you visions of paid-off mortgages dancing in your head.

You have to admit, these guys are good at what they do. They could charm persimmons out of an opossum's paws. But don't ever fall for their claims. Don't recommend that your pastor or congregation get involved, either. And don't give them my name just to get them off your back and out of your office.

Sheepdogs Among the Flock

One of the very worst things a ministry leader can do is to recommend investments to those in their church—unless they are a certified financial planner or investment counselor. Because when this scam falls apart, as it surely will, people won't be angry with the scam artist. They'll be angry with their leaders, whose advice they trusted enough to risk—and lose—their money.

What about *people who are involved in sin*? I have saved this one for last, because these are actually among the easiest cases to correct. When a believer is involved in sin, you have a written instruction manual to guide you—it's called the Bible. Your mission in these situations is to point out what the Word of God says and tell the one who is sinning that their responsibility is to repent and change their behavior to line up with what God clearly expects of them. If they are in any kind of leadership position, there should be some consequence to their actions. Every local church should develop a procedure to follow in these circumstances.

If the wrongdoing has been committed by a staff member, you will need competent legal advice to make sure you are following due process, and that you limit the legal exposure such a situation may create. There should also be a written employee manual that covers the procedures that must be followed.

There are two main problems that arise in dealing with people who are in sin. The first is when a controversy devolves into an adversarial confrontation between an accuser and the accused, and there is not a preponderance of evidence for either point of view. God's wisdom is needed in these cases, and it is readily available to all leaders who ask for it with a pure motive.

The second is when the one involved in sin refuses to admit their guilt, and does everything to try to rationalize and make excuses for their behavior, denying any wrongdoing and accusing everyone else of having an unjustified vendetta against them. In the event the evidence is incontrovertible, the consequences need to be carried out as quickly and privately as possible, so that the damage from their behavior can be minimized, and repentance and restoration can occur sooner rather than later.

As you can see, being a sheepdog isn't all about talking to angels and singing God's praises. Sometimes you have to deal with Sister Bess and Brother Jess and their big mess. But be encouraged, because God will anoint you to do this just as much as He will enable you to accomplish the more pleasant functions that are part of working with the people God has given into your care.

CHAPTER 17

Talent or Character?

One of the things that characterizes the present age is the fascination many people have with those who have attained celebrity status. There are magazines and television programs devoted to nothing more than letting us know what is going on in the private lives of those who have become famous. We are bombarded on a daily basis with information about people who have achieved notoriety in the areas of entertainment, professional sports or business. Those who can make us laugh or cry, provide products or services efficiently, throw a ball through a hoop or carry one across a goal line become heroes, making truckloads of money and garnering lots of attention.

Many (but by no means all) of these people are brilliantly, even astonishingly talented, which is often the thing that enables them to be celebrities in the first place. Many of them work hard at what they do, but to most ordinary folks who are unaware of what happens behind the glitz and glamour, it appears that their success was given to them, and they seem to enjoy the good life without much effort.

Sheepdogs Among the Flock

The gossip columns and tabloid programs are full of reports of unusual and even bizarre behavior from celebrities. In many cases, these same people who acquire the most accolades have the hardest time maintaining their money, their relationships or their reputations. A higher than average proportion of them develop destructive lifestyles, have difficulty maintaining harmonious relationships or become involved in addictive behaviors that would not be tolerated in those who have less money or fame. They have truly become the gods of this age.

CHARACTER IS IRREPLACEABLE

Unfortunately, this attitude of idolizing talent and minimizing character has crept into the body of Christ.

Make no mistake, I thank God for the talented individuals who fulfill so many tasks in the church. It seems as though every day someone new comes along with abilities and gifts that God is using mightily. But before we get too enamored with the abilities people have, we must not fail to examine a principle that has often been overlooked—and that is character.

There is no doubt that a certain level of talent is required in the kingdom of God, especially for certain functions. But when it comes to being a sheepdog, I have always maintained that talent is not as important as character. You may have the greatest gift, or talent, in the world when it comes to playing an instrument, singing, preaching or anything else that requires talent. But what good is all that ability if you never show up on time to use what God has given you?

There was one man I knew who was the absolute best at what he did. I have never seen anyone better. Unfortunately, he was seldom on time. He was a genius in his field, but unreliable when it came to timeliness. His great gift was rendered ineffective because of his inconsistency.

Talent is not the key to being used by God—and the church should never be regarded as an audition hall for your special skill. There are many people who have loads of talent, but God doesn't use them. In fact, there are people sitting on bar stools who have far more talent than some who are nationally known, but their talent isn't helping them to be useful in His kingdom.

I believe the key to being used by God is not *talent*, but *character*. Character has nothing to do with a gift you have received, but has everything to do with having the fruit of the Spirit developed in your life.

On Christmas morning, kids assemble in front of the tree to find all the packages with their names on them. They unwrap all their gifts, play with them a while and then look for something else to do. The gifts they receive have little if anything to do with their character. They don't get gifts based on whether they deserve them or even need them—they get them on the basis of grace and the goodwill of their parents.

Character is different. It doesn't come fully grown, but is developed through a multitude of different experiences, not all of them pleasant. Character is much more representative than talent of who a person really is and how effective they can be.

Here's another example to illustrate the difference. Christmas is a time of celebration, and many families have a tradition of obtaining a live evergreen tree for the holiday season. Sometimes they even go to a tree farm and cut the tree down themselves. They bring it home, set it up and hang beautiful decorations on it. Those are gifts. They are beautiful, but not natural. They catch our attention, but don't last very long. Someone has to put them on the outside of the tree—and when the holiday is over, they go back in a box or a bin to be brought out the next time they are needed.

Other things may be growing on the same tree called pine cones. They don't look very attractive, but they are important, since they contain the tree's seeds. They are not gifts, but fruit. They do not come from without, but from within, and are representative of the life that is in the tree. They may not be as shiny or attract as much attention as the gifts, but they occur naturally, and if given proper care will produce many more just like themselves.

That is why I believe fruit is much more important than gifts when it comes to being a sheepdog. Gifts are certainly helpful, even essential, but character is irreplaceable. And there is one characteristic that is more valuable than any other in qualifying ministry helpers for effective service.

FAITHFULNESS IS REQUIRED

Paul said in 1 Corinthians 4:2: *"Moreover it is required in stewards that a man be found faithful."*

A steward is someone who does not own, but only manages. Sheepdogs don't own people or churches, but are managers and helpers in those things which belong to the Lord and are under the guidance of a shepherd. The characteristic that God looks for more than any other in a ministry helper is faithfulness. Another way to describe it is reliability.

A fundamental area where sheepdogs must prove their trustworthiness is regarding money. We must never forget that the resources of a church come from people who have worked, sweated and sacrificed to provide what is needed. The money you spend is their life. If it is not used to rescue someone else's life in some way, it is being wasted. God may be extravagant, but He is never wasteful, and He is not pleased with His stewards being overly indulgent or wasteful, either.

Whenever you are spending someone else's money, treat it as though you were spending yours. Perhaps I should rephrase that, because some people have no sense or restraint when it comes to spending money. I hope they are not on the staff of your church.

Be responsible. Keep records and receipts. Reconcile your accounts as soon as you get back from wherever you have gone on church business. If you have lost money or receipts, you should make it up from your own funds, and do it without hesitation. If you hold yourself to this standard, you will think twice before being careless with what belongs to someone else.

Jesus told a story about an unjust steward in Luke chapter 16. This man said he was too weak to dig and too ashamed to beg. He had a lot of experience when it came to stealing, though. (If thieves would work as hard at honest labor as they do trying to defraud others, nobody could keep them from achieving legitimate wealth.) This man's lord told him he would have to give an account of his stewardship—the day of reckoning finally came.

We will all give an account of our stewardship before the throne of God, and He keeps accurate records. Heaven is not populated with unrepentant embezzlers and fraudulent schemers.

As a sheepdog among the flock, people will give you money all the time for all sorts of reasons. Maybe they missed the offering and want you to make sure it gets included. Perhaps it is a gift they want to pass on to someone you will see, but they will not encounter. They may want to remain anonymous, and ask you to discreetly get it into the proper hands. You have no business being in any kind of authority in any area of God's house if you will not be faithful and responsible about handling money.

Jesus said that money was among the least of things over which we would exercise stewardship. Many people act as though it is the greatest of things. How different God's perspective is than ours. I believe that money is not just a means of exchange, but in many cases, it is also a test of faithfulness. I have seen people disqualify themselves from greater usefulness in God's kingdom by not only being covetous, but also by being careless with money. If money can pass through your hands without sticking to your fingers, and if you are accountable to God and man for how you use it, you won't have to worry about God's willingness to bless you. He will be able to trust you, not only with money, but with His people.

Sheepdogs must demonstrate trustworthiness and reliability, because the shepherd leaves them with the sheep. There is no greater treasure in God's kingdom than His people. People are our greatest resource, and their care is our most noble calling besides our adoration of God Himself. Here is the measure of importance God gave to those He created—He sent Jesus to die for them. We must be faithful to provide the care they need.

The opposite of faithfulness is to be untrustworthy. Proverbs has quite a few things to say about unfaithful servants, none of them complimentary.

In ancient times, bow making was a highly-prized skill. A good bow was a lethal weapon and was used to keep enemies at a distance. From time to time, instead of bending the right way, the limbs of a few bows would fail and turn backward, endangering the shooter instead of the target. These bows were called unfaithful, since they could not be trusted to fulfill their intended purpose.

Sheepdogs Among the Flock

In the same way, an unreliable sheepdog is useless, since he can no longer be trusted with the sheep. God will not hold us guiltless if we fail to fulfill our responsibility to the sheep He has put in our keeping.

A primary principle of the kingdom of God is that faithfulness is rewarded. However, in some cases in the church, faithfulness is overlooked in favor of other characteristics, such as money, talent or notoriety.

The Bible makes it clear that novices are not to be placed in positions of responsibility, and yet we see this happen every time a baby Christian who happens to be well-known in some field of worldly endeavor is given a microphone and a pulpit. Our collective heads are turned by the fame they have obtained, and we expect to receive something of value from them. How much better it would be if they had someone over them who was not starry-eyed over their celebrity status, but would instead take them in as a new convert and give them the same training and instruction that is available to others. What a blessing they would be to the cause of Christ if this were to happen.

Some obtain special status because of their large financial contributions or long-standing family influence in a local body of believers. James 2 warns against favoring the rich because of their wealth. The church is not a country club, where membership or status is determined by a big donation or the referral of a family member. Everyone in the church becomes a member on the same basis—being born again through faith in the blood of Jesus Christ shed on the cross. And everyone is qualified for promotion on the basis of how faithfully they serve in the area where God assigns them.

Just because someone has fortune and fame doesn't mean they are ready to preach—or to do anything else in the house of God. They should be ready to learn, and if they don't have the right attitude, they should never get near a pulpit or position of leadership until that is worked out in them. Of course, this scenario doesn't just happen with those who are rich and famous—it can happen with anyone.

DEALING WITH LESS TALENTED, BUT FAITHFUL HELPERS

There are many honest, compassionate and hardworking believers in churches all over the world who don't have a lot of talent, but they are willing to use whatever they have to bless someone else. But when someone comes along who is perceived as having more talent in a certain area, they are given the opportunity to do what the faithful believer has been laboring over, sometimes for years. In many cases, the talented one is put in a position of authority over the faithful volunteer who has been working in that area. This can cause distress if it isn't managed properly.

One problem arises when the talented one does not take the time to get to know those with whom they are working, but comes into the situation with a superior attitude. They are not willing to learn from or listen to others, because they perceive they know it all because of their gift, or because of previous experiences their gift gave them elsewhere. This can create hard feelings among those who have worked diligently to develop the program or procedure that has been used in the past and is now being changed or completely discarded, sometimes without any explanation.

A new staff member was tasked with the responsibility for guest relations for special meetings. This person was familiar with many of the ministry guests who came to the church for these occasions, and felt that it would be better to use a system they brought with them from another place instead of finding out how things were done where they were presently. It would be kind to describe the result as chaotic.

More often than not, the talented ones regard themselves as the next apostle Paul and come in with a gangbuster attitude. They may not have learned how to be a servant to those they perceive are under them, or how to submit to others, or how to deal graciously with those who disagree with them. When things don't go their way, they blow up and threaten to quit. This produces even more instability in an already difficult situation.

What causes this to happen so often in churches? Usually it is because the pastor, or other leader, is so challenged and overwhelmed by the pressures of ministry they seek those they think can give them help in a particular area right away. Sometimes other considerations diminish in importance and are allowed to fall by the wayside. When promotion comes as a result of talent rather than character, problems always result.

Talent or Character?

LOYALTY IS ESSENTIAL

There are lots of faithful sheepdogs out there, serving with distinction. Stability is one of the characteristics others should be able to see in you as a faithful helper.

The loyalty factor among natural sheepdogs is high. They tend to spend many years faithfully serving in the same sheepfold. I have always wondered why so many helpers in Christian ministry seem to have difficulty staying put. I am convinced one reason the body of Christ is so split and splintered is because we have not allowed God to keep us in one place long enough to develop the kinds of relationships that are necessary to build anything lasting.

When I first became involved in ministry, I had the opportunity to become friends with a group of people in a small community who later started a local church. At one point before the church began, they were meeting together regularly when some problem arose. I remember thinking that the entire group was in danger of fracturing because of the issue.

As I heard them talk about how they resolved the problem, they kept referring to the long-term relationships they had with one another. They met, talked and prayed together. Eventually the problem was resolved with no hurt feelings, no offense and no compromising the work that God intended to raise up among them.

I was a young man when this happened, and some of these people had known one another longer than I had been alive. It made quite an impression on me that they would not allow a relatively serious disagreement come between them because they had already made such an investment in one another's lives. They had a measure of trust and good-will that amazed me, and would not have been possible had they not known one another for so long.

Don't be in a hurry to use your gifts elsewhere. Allow God to do the work in you He may not be able to do if you are always jumping from place to place. Don't look at your helping as another way to get your ticket punched or your resume enhanced to go on to the next level of ministry, whatever that is.

We need to have more of the character of the badger than the bumblebee. The bee flits from place to place, always seeking out the brightest flowers and the sweetest nec-tar. Badgers, on the other hand, tend to stay in one place and stake their claim regardless of what comes. Badgers hold on.

There is no doubt that some people are called to a place for a specific season. Our ministry deals with lots of Bible college students, who tend to be in one location only long enough to complete their course of study before God moves them on to their next assignment. This is as it should be, but I hope that before long they will find a place that will be right for them for many years to come.

There are those whose calling involves traveling. This, too, is part of a genuine equipping that fills a legitimate need in the body of Christ. Traveling ministry may seem glamorous, but anyone who tells you they really enjoy it falls into one of two categories: they are genuinely called to it, or they have never done it.

Regardless of how far you fare, you need to have a home church. Every bird has a roost, whether they are homebodies or world travelers. Every ship, no matter how far it sails, has a home port. Allow God to establish you in a place where you are at home, and where your brothers and sisters welcome you home.

WATCH OUT FOR THE HIRELING

Jesus gave the characteristics of a hireling in John 10:12-13. In contrast to the shepherd, the hireling flees when danger threatens, because he doesn't care for the sheep, but only cares for himself. He is in the business for what he can get out of it. He is more interested in his paycheck, his benefits and his vacation days than making sure the sheep are cared for and kept safe. Hirelings are not sheepdogs at all—they're just ordinary dogs that cause more trouble than they are worth. They have no business being anywhere near the sheep.

I was involved in the interview process with a man who was applying for a ministry position. We asked him to describe his daily schedule, and he told us what he did on a typical weekday. It sounded like he was on perpetual vacation at an island resort. He asked us about our typical weekday schedule, so we described it to him in unembellished detail. We never heard from him again.

Sheepdogs Among the Flock

One way to find out whether a person has a mercenary mentality is to watch how they interact with people—but not the people who will be over them. It is to their advantage to make a good impression on leadership. Take notice of how they treat those who will not be able to do anything for them. Their attitude and demeanor around the "ordinary" people will tell you a lot about their character.

A highly-touted candidate tried out for a ministry position. During his visit, he met a number of people who were important to the proper functioning of the church, but who did not tell him what they did. He treated them with disdain, and even contempt. He seemed to think they were beneath him. We thanked him for coming, sent him on his way, and never talked to him again.

If you would like to test this with someone you suspect of having a hireling point of view, ask someone they do not know and would not be able to recognize to arrange some interaction with them. If the prospective employee does not give them the time of day, you probably won't want them in any kind of position of responsibility with the sheep. On the other hand, if they are gracious and warm to those people, chances are that's the way they will conduct themselves with everyone.

From time to time, the shepherd may find it necessary to obtain the services of someone who can do what none of the sheepdogs are able to do. In today's specialized and compartmentalized world, some specific tasks need to be handled by specialists in those fields. Areas where technical expertise or licensing requirements are needed may result in having staff members who may not be in tune with the shepherd when it comes to personal interaction with the sheep, but whose skills in their areas of service give them unique qualifications to do a certain essential job.

Many times, these people are results-oriented in a people business, and this causes some difficulties when it comes to keeping the flock encouraged and headed in the right direction. If their influence is not tempered by care and concern, the sheep can become confused and scattered. Over the years I have often had to rub some oil on a sheep that had been bruised by some sort of conflict with an extremely talented individual—it's just that their talents didn't include ministering to people in a consistently compassionate way.

In my experience, it is best to limit these especially talented folks' exposure to the flock as a whole and allow them to fulfill their calling in their area of expertise. Just because someone is gifted in some specialized area doesn't mean they should have liberty to roam at will with the flock.

On one occasion, we had a staff member gifted in a technical area who couldn't be found at certain times of the day. We later discovered that during these times, he was talking to ministry supporters about a business scheme he was developing, and he was soliciting their financial involvement.

On a few other occasions, staff people would use special services with visiting ministries as their chance to lobby for job opportunities elsewhere. This is purest folly, and anyone who would hire someone who would do such a thing deserves the kind of help they get from such people. They are not sheepdogs, but mercenaries and hired guns. When they think there is a chance for more money or less responsibility somewhere else, they jump ship and head out for the next port with some other crew. May they find what they seek far away.

As Ecclesiastes 12:13 says, *"Let us hear the conclusion of the matter...."* Talent will not take you the distance in this race. You cannot build people, or a ministry, on a gift. Your gift or ability may be honed to a keen edge, but if you have neglected building godly character into your life, I can promise you that disaster is down the road. Don't let your talent take you where your character can't keep you.

I am not trying to convince you that a choice must be made between either possessing talent or having character. We need both to fulfill God's purposes. You may be gifted in a supernatural way, and you should do your best to refine and use that gift for the glory of God. However, I will caution you to remember that your possession of a gift from God does not mean that you have the character of God developed in you.

It takes discipline and passion to develop a gift—but character is developed the same way and has the same requirements. The difference is that character is not given from without, but it lies deep within, and has a greater reward.

CHAPTER 18

Wolves Among the Sheep

I'm sure you remember the story of Little Red Riding Hood's visit to her grandmother's house. When she arrived at granny's bedside, she noticed something wasn't quite right about her, and commented on her unusual appearance. I never remember Red being described as the sharpest kid in the storybook, but she surely should have recognized something was wrong with her grandmother. Of course, it was really the wolf trying to impersonate the old woman in order to get its fangs into the little girl. That's the problem with wolves—they have no scruples, either in bedtime stories or in spiritual matters.

I have no axe to grind against wolves in their natural environment—they are top-shelf predators, extraordinarily adapted for the role they play in the wild. But as any sheep rancher knows, sheep and wolves don't get along well together, and the sheep always lose in a head-to-head encounter.

GET TO KNOW THE SHEEP

Just as Little Red Riding Hood should have been able to recognize the wolf, sheepdogs should be able to spot one immediately. You might think the best way to do this is to spend a lot of time studying wolves, but that would distract the sheepdog from keeping his eye on the sheep. The surest way to recognize a wolf is to recognize what isn't a sheep.

One of my daughters spent some time as a customer service representative at a local bank. One day the bank received a notice that some counterfeit twenty-dollar bills were circulating in the community, and that all CSR's should be aware of any suspicious-looking ones.

I asked her how they watched for fake bills. I imagined that they went over the characteristics of the counterfeit money in great detail, explaining what to expect. She said that they did describe the details of what the fakes looked like, but that wasn't their first line of defense.

What the bank depended on most was the employee's familiarity with genuine money. My daughter explained that in handling money day after day, they became so familiar with the real thing that when anything out of the ordinary came through their hands, most of the time they would notice it immediately. It was only after a bill had been flagged that they would give it more careful scrutiny to find the specific things that were not right about it.

I understand that people are infinitely more intricate and individual than dollar bills, but there is something to be said for becoming familiar with the characteristics of sheep.

I grew up around farmers who raised sheep. On a few occasions, my cousin and I raised orphaned lambs whose mothers had either died or rejected them. I have had the privilege of seeing sheep being sheared, wormed, docked, born, raised, fed and just about everything else that can be done with them. They are fascinating creatures. I recommend that every sheepdog have a chance to observe the four-legged kind of sheep. It will help them become more compassionate toward the human kind.

Sheep are not sharp in any sense of the word. They are not the smartest animal God created. I was in a conversation with a sheep farmer after a church service one evening, and he said, "You can have a flock of a hundred sheep, and if you don't take care of them, in a year's time there won't be any left. They'll wander off, get sick, die of exposure or get eaten."

Sheepdogs, please listen: sheep require a lot of attention.

Sheep are round. Their eyes are round. Their behinds are round. Their muzzles and noses are round. Their shoulders and hooves and even their teeth are rounded. They are made for neither speed nor distance. Their safety is in numbers, and in the constant care of the shepherd and his helpers.

Wolves, on the other hand, are not round, but angular. They have long legs, long tails, long jaws and long teeth. About the only similarities between them and sheep are that they are both mammals that have four legs and a tail.

I have seen sheep in conflict with each other. They kick with their feet, butt with their heads, and shove with their shoulders. I watched one afternoon as the farmer was throwing hay down into a hay rack, and two sheep were determined to put their heads into the same stanchion. They shoved and butted and kicked so long that the others ate nearly all the hay before those two finally decided that eating was preferable to fighting.

I have had lambs suck my fingers, young and old sheep alike eat things out of my hands, and have pulled back their lips to inspect their gums and teeth. I have never been bitten intentionally by a sheep, and I have never seen sheep bite one another. It may happen, but if it does, it is rare. If you are observing what looks like a sheep engaging in uncharacteristic behavior by biting another sheep, you may have discovered a wolf in sheep's clothing. Remember Little Red Riding Hood and her inquiry about her grandmother's teeth?

Another characteristic you should always remember about sheep is that they are group animals. It is unusual to see a sheep by itself. This happens most often when it is about to give birth, or is sick, injured, lost, terrified or otherwise stressed. The rest of the time they stay with the group. As a sheepdog, you may grow weary of rounding up strays, but that is part of your job. The true shepherd is more concerned about the one who is lost than the ninety-nine who are safe.

PREDATORS SPREAD FALSE DOCTRINE

In Acts 20, the apostle Paul spoke earnestly to the elders of the church at Ephesus on his way back to Jerusalem after his third missionary journey. He warned them that grievous wolves would enter in among them, not sparing the flock.

How could this happen? Ephesus was probably the focus of more of Paul's labor than any other city he visited in his lifetime. If any church received his personal attention and a strong start, it was the one at Ephesus. What went wrong?

Obviously, someone was not paying attention. Paul spoke to the elders of the church, telling them that men would arise from their midst, speaking perverse things in order to draw away disciples after themselves.

This gives us another look at what wolves do. They spread false doctrine in an effort to separate the flock, and cause schism and division. This is something for which the faithful sheepdog needs to watch. He should sound the alarm immediately if he sees it starting.

The biggest problem with this is, as Paul said, that wolves sometimes arise among the leadership of the flock. This makes it doubly difficult for a sheepdog to point out the error, since the wolf is someone that the sheep already know and trust.

I remember several occasions over the years where those known and trusted by the sheep began to develop an agenda radically different from that of the shepherd. Their folly was not recognized at first, and only became clear after some of the sheep had already been drawn away and damaged.

Sheepdogs Among the Flock

False doctrine doesn't only mean that someone starts preaching heresy—it can also mean someone begins advocating a position or point of view that is in opposition to the vision of the local church. We don't have to agree about every single thing, but there cannot be two visions in one house. More than *one vision* inevitably leads to *di-vision*, and the consequences are disastrous.

In 1 Corinthians 1:10, Paul admonished the church at Corinth that:

> *...you all speak in agreement and that there be no divisions among you. But be perfectly joined together in the same mind and in the same judgment.*

We can't be saying the same thing if we are hearing opposing voices and following leaders who are going in opposite directions.

If what leaders do is so important, how can we make sure that those in leadership continue leading in a redemptive way? Shepherds need to trust their helpers, give them responsibility, and let them grow and develop—even if it involves making mistakes. Shepherds also need to keep an eye on the helpers, while keeping a finger on the pulse of the congregation. False doctrine is much more easily corrected before it is fully developed.

One of our neighbors had a wet spot in their backyard. Regardless of how dry the weather was, it always remained moist. In an effort to correct this, they planted a very fast-growing tree in the middle of the damp place. It was no more than a stick when they first planted it, but it grew very rapidly, and was eventually taller than their house.

They began to wonder what would happen if the tree blew over in a storm. They contemplated cutting it down. By that time, the tree had grown so large that it would take specialized equipment and a great deal of expense to get rid of it. Shortly after it was planted, however, anyone could have pulled it out of the ground with one hand.

Jesus talked about how a grain of mustard seed, the smallest of seeds, would soon become a tree that was so large birds could lodge in its branches. He also warned His disciples to beware of leaven. He wasn't talking about bread, but about false and damaging doctrine. Leaven works quietly, silently and completely, and before long it will work its way through an entire batch of dough—or an entire body of believers. Keep an eye and ear out for false doctrine.

As a faithful ministry helper, you may be able to recognize false doctrine, but how do you expect the sheep to know it when it comes their way? My recommendation is that the church and all of its functions be built upon doctrine that is clearly articulated and circulated among the congregation. This can happen in a new members' class, in small groups or even in pulpit ministry. Let God give you wisdom about how to make what you believe and why you believe it known to everyone in your fellowship. Consider the time and effort spent doing this as an insurance policy for your church body.

Sheepdogs Among the Flock

PREDATORS ARE OPPORTUNISTS

One of the characteristics of predators such as wolves is that they are opportunists, picking out the animals that are the most vulnerable first. Any sheep that is lame, sick, weak or has some other condition that makes it look or act differently from the rest can be easy prey for the wolf.

Spiritual wolves also look for their victims in the form of people who are stressed, unhappy, bound by habits or addictions, or otherwise unable to connect completely and in a fulfilling manner with a body of believers. These also happen to be the people who are most likely to be on the fringes of the fellowship and may be overlooked when it comes to receiving enough attention from the shepherd and his helpers. Sometimes their absence is not noticed as soon as the absence of others who may be more regularly involved in the life of the church.

Wolves may not be much of a problem for a church that is small and has the full focus of the pastor or other leaders. But when a flock grows quickly, is unusually large, or involves many facets of ministry, it creates momentum that attracts lots of attention—and not all the attention is helpful.

In the wild, wolves have home ranges, but they may be very large, and they will travel long distances to make a kill. Some wolves don't belong to a pack or family group, but are on their own. These loners come out of nowhere to slash and slay before moving on as quickly as they came.

We should always welcome visitors to our congregations and our communities. After all, we want everyone to hear the gospel message. But, sooner or later, there will be someone who will come to town or through the front door who is interested in the body for the wrong reasons. It takes a discerning heart to know when someone has a motive that is contrary to the purpose of the church. I don't recommend that we have a spirit of suspicion, but we need to be aware that everyone doesn't come to church for the same reasons we do.

Decades ago, someone who called himself an evangelist came to our city and set up shop in a well-known venue. Before long, word got around that he was having meetings where the supernatural was in manifestation every night. Some of the people in the church wanted to go to the meetings, so Pastor Parsley asked two of us on the church staff to attend a service and check it out.

Elmer Gantry had nothing on this guy. He was clever. I heard more innuendo and suggestion in that meeting than could be found on a psychic hot line. He would ask people questions about themselves and then tell them something he would have no natural way of knowing—or so it seemed.

When we described to our pastor what we had seen and heard, he told us the minister was employing two of the most elementary tactics used by wolves everywhere to pull the wool over unsuspecting sheep's eyes. One of this man's claims was that he could tell people their names, addresses and other facts about them. There is no doubt that God can show His servants anything about anyone at any time—but God always does it for a redemptive purpose.

Sheepdogs Among the Flock

One deceptive strategy that is sometimes used to convince people that someone is hearing from God is to send surrogates out into the crowd before a meeting starts who will greet people, talk to them, and make note of certain things about them. Then, before the minister comes out, they will tell him where these people are sitting, describe them, and tell him what they have learned. When the minister repeats this information to the unsuspecting people, it seems supernatural, but it isn't at all. (If I come up to talk to you before a service, feel confident about responding. I will never do what I have just described.)

Another way unscrupulous preachers can get information from people is by having a television camera focus on them to obtain their names or other information from the front of their Bibles, a name tag, or even a checkbook or offering envelope. Once again, this information can be conveyed to the minister, who calls someone out and tells them what he has learned. Most of the time, the person on the receiving end of this "ministry" will assume it is God that spoke to the minister about them.

Pastor Parsley explained these same tactics in church that Sunday morning to help our congregation understand just what was happening. He cautioned them that if they wanted to know their name and address, they didn't need to go to some little-known preacher's meeting in a dusty hall somewhere. All they had to do was consult their driver's license.

Please don't think that I'm saying that most traveling evangelists or television ministers are slick-haired, shiny-shoed hucksters. The vast majority of ministers are some of the hardest-working, most morally upright people you will ever know. But that doesn't mean we can ignore those who try to use the pulpit to increase their own fame and wealth, instead of edifying the body of Christ. Paul warned us about these people. So did John. So did Jude. So did Jesus. Sheep-dogs everywhere should take note.

How to Tell If a Sheep Has Been Torn

What happens to people who have been infected with false doctrine, or who have had questions placed in their mind by wolves about the sincerity and trustworthiness of their church leaders? Here are some telling characteristics.

Sometimes you will notice people who start out on fire—always there, in the front, excited, and endeavoring to be involved in everything they can. At some point, you notice you don't see them as often any more. Maybe they don't sit in the front, but are about halfway back. Then they come late, sit in the back, and leave early. Then they disappear. What has happened to them?

There are no simple answers, since there may be a multitude of reasons why a particular individual or family stops coming to church. One reason may be that the wolf has bitten them, and they have simply disappeared.

Sometimes sheep become discouraged about their role in the church or in the kingdom of God, and there will be occasions when this discouragement is due directly to the influence of a wolf filling them with false doctrine or misleading information that causes their fire to grow dim.

Sometimes people who are getting along just fine grow suspicious and critical. Nothing pleases them any longer, and they spread discontent to all those around them. This may be due to the wolf biting and slashing at decisions that have been made by those in leadership.

There will be times when there are sheep that just fall by the wayside and stop following the Lord altogether. They have grown cold, have no testimony of faith, and no longer walk with the Lord. This could also be the work of the wolf, that always comes to steal, kill and destroy.

DEALING WITH THE WOLF

What do you do about a wolf that is causing problems among the sheep? They must be confronted quickly and decisively. Most of the time, they will leave in a hurry if they are exposed. This should be done privately, since there is no need or benefit in disturbing the flock about it, except in the most serious of circumstances. If the wolf doesn't get out after that, you still have alternatives. The most effective one is to ask God to move them out. He will. I've seen it happen time and time again.

Another minister accompanied me to confront a wolf who was one of the meanest and most contrary individuals I have ever met. He would sit in church services and mock what was going on, to the point where he would distract those who sat around him. We had to speak to him sitting in a pew before a service, since he would not agree to meet with us in a private setting. He ridiculed our counsel, refused to acknowledge our right to ask anything of him, and remained adamant that he was not doing anything wrong. He reminded me of Nabal, who was described this way in 1 Samuel 25:17: *"He is such a worthless man that one cannot speak to him."*

"What are we going to do?" my colleague asked me.

"We're going to ask God to get him out of here," I said.

We prayed about it right then. The man only came to one more service before his job transferred him out of town, and we never saw him again.

COYOTES

Wolves are not the only ones that cause problems among the flock. Others can raise havoc, too. I call them *wannabe wolves* or *coyotes*.

Once confined to the west, coyotes have proliferated in unbelievable numbers in many areas far from their ancestral home. When natural prey is not abundant, they make the necessary adjustments to survive by eating garbage, pet food or anything else they can find. They hide in the most unusual places, and they are infinitely subtle and sneaky. Some Native Americans regard the coyote as the ultimate trickster—a reputation well-deserved.

As homes continue to be built in outlying reaches of urban areas, human and coyote conflict is becoming more common. One suburban dweller had just let her little dog out for a run in the fenced backyard. Imagine her horror when a coyote came up from the aqueduct behind her house, bounded over the chain link fence, snatched up her pooch and returned the way it came, disappearing without a trace.

Coyotes in the church behave in exactly the same way.

There will be occasions when people arrive at your church with a lot of fanfare about how glad they are to be there and how committed they are to the vision of the house. This is a great thing if it is genuine. It is a dangerous thing if it is not.

A family came to our church and immediately pitched in to help wherever they could. They had a heartbreaking story of hardship. They continually assured us that they felt they had found a home in our church, and they wanted to be a blessing in any way they could. But something about their situation didn't seem right to the leadership, and we watched them closely.

It wasn't long before problems began to arise. The husband couldn't find a job. The wife had many physical problems for which there seemed to be no medical explanations. They were expecting a large inheritance that would provide for them, but it was long overdue. In the meantime, could the church—or someone—take care of the utility bills, or next month's rent?

The clincher came one day when the family came to the leadership with a terrible problem. They claimed they had lost a large amount of money somewhere in the building. They had planned to use it the next day to pay all their urgent bills, but it had mysteriously disappeared. Surely the church had an insurance policy to deal with these kinds of things, and they wanted to file a claim. (No such claim was filed. Insurance fraud is a crime.)

The last time we saw these folks, they were driving a moving truck to their next destination. It was full of furniture, appliances, and other belongings they had acquired from well-meaning and tenderhearted people in our church and other churches who wanted to relieve what they thought was the distress of a family who needed their help. Even though these people were not wolves, they were certainly coyotes, snatching whatever they could and running off with it before they could be caught.

Unfortunately, there are times when depredations by predators will happen even in the best sheepfolds. Our commitment as those who guard the sheep must be to provide the most consistent and vigilant oversight possible, so the flock can flourish in green pastures beside still waters. As we fulfill our ministry of watching and protecting, we can be encouraged by knowing that the Great Shepherd watches over and protects us all.

CHAPTER 19

Common Ailments
of the Sheepdog

One of the most unsavory tasks we had as dog owners was to worm them. The thought of worms infesting our hounds' digestive tracts was disgusting, but the dogs had to be treated regularly to keep them healthy. We would do all kinds of things to persuade the dogs to swallow the worm pills, which they were understandably reluctant to do. It was necessary—although quite an ordeal—because worms are a common problem with dogs everywhere.

In the same way, sheepdogs among the flock have common ailments. In the process of ministering, faithful helpers can pick up some parasitic conditions that will sap their spiritual strength and limit their effectiveness.

RECOVERING FROM MISTAKES

Despite how much confidence ministry helpers project, two things that trouble them most consistently are doubt and discouragement. I'm not talking about doubting God's

Word, but the kinds of doubts that come from wondering if they are pleasing those to whom they respond and report. Internal concerns about their performance can degrade their capability, and in seasons when they have little contact with the shepherd, they will have to work hard to find reasons to stay encouraged about the job they are doing.

This can be especially troublesome if they are new to their tasks or have not had the time to develop a confident relationship with their pastor. A probationary period can be very stressful for a helper who is eager to please, but who recognizes his limitations and deficiencies. When the devil's accusations are added to all this, it can create a toxic atmosphere that will poison a sheepdog's self-esteem.

Most of the time, busy pastors are self-motivated, and do not need people to continuously tell them that they are doing a good job in order to stay focused. They may not realize that their helpers need this kind of consistent affirmation.

Sheepdogs need to know they are doing the right things the right way. A word in season will bring joy to their hearts and a smile to their countenances. This does not mean that a shepherd can never bring correction without ruining all the helpers, but a smile and a few kind words from the shepherd are pure gold to the trusting sheepdog.

What if you blow it? What if you have really made a mess of things: the project is not completed, the assignment is not done right, or the results you have produced are only a fraction of what was expected? What if your efforts, or lack of them, have created such a problem, cost the ministry so much money, or missed such a great opportunity that the shepherd becomes angry?

The best thing you can do when faced with the righteous wrath of a wronged shepherd is to stay in your place, admit your fault and refuse to make excuses. Own your mistakes. Avoid casting accusations at others for your own shortcomings. Let your *yes* be *yes* and your *no* be *no*. If you don't know the answers to questions, don't try to backpedal and befog the situation with terms such as *if I had known* and *I didn't realize.* The end of a failed project is not the time to admit you didn't know what to do, how to do it or by when it needed to be done.

Failure is not final—nor is it an opportunity to blame others for your pain so you can justify doing things the next time exactly as you did them the last time. You need to make progress from where you are, especially if that is a place of abject failure. Don't lick your wounds, rehearse your hurts and nurse your grudges. Improvement will inevitably involve self-evaluation and change—sometimes radical change. Make the changes. Do it.

AVOID COMPARISONS

One of the biggest pitfalls a sheepdog must avoid is comparing himself with the capabilities and performance of other sheepdogs. As the flock grows, other sheepdogs will surely be needed to help with the sheep, and all those involved in the cause of Christ must refuse the temptation to become involved in comparing their respective merits or faults with one another. A spirit of envy has no place among the servants of the Lord.

We see this demonstrated among Jesus' disciples when they began to strive about which of them should be the greatest. Jesus Himself ended the debate by telling them the true measure of greatness is serving, not being served. The entire episode is recorded in Luke 22:24-27 and should be read regularly by every ministry helper.

If we find our satisfaction in being the very best at what we do, what will happen when someone comes along who can do what we do better than we do it? What we should do in such a case is celebrate a brother or sister's accomplishments. But what we often do in real life is try to find a way to sabotage their efforts, denigrate their accomplishments and try to make ourselves look good in comparison to them.

My sense of fulfillment must never be in knowing that there is nobody better than me. When it comes to my work, it's probably not true. There is nothing wrong with having a fire and a determination to do things with excellence — there has been too much mediocrity in the body of Christ. But if my desire to excel causes me to become involved in strife, debate and schism, then I have gone too far in the wrong direction and for the wrong reasons.

If all I can do is climb the ladder of success, knocking everyone ahead of me off, it won't be too long after I've reached the top that I will be expending more effort trying to resist being kicked off the highest rung than I will accomplishing my purpose. How is that any different than the world's system that I am commanded to forswear?

If I really want to achieve success, I have to become focused on someone besides myself. Dr. Lester Sumrall spent decades of his life investing in young men and women in ministry, helping them become successes of their own. My pastor does it. One of the most rewarding things I have done in ministry is to teach young men and women principles of ministry in both formal and informal settings. One of the greatest thrills I have is to hear stories of their achievements. I hope they all become better at what they do than I am at what I do. My life is not diminished by their success; it is magnified.

None of us are going to last forever. If Jesus does not return in my lifetime, I can think of nothing more rewarding than to have someone I have had a chance to influence take my place and go far beyond anything I have done.

Jesus said in John 14:12: *"…he who believes in Me will do the works that I do also. And he will do greater works than these, because I am going to My Father."*

He didn't say, "You'll never do more than I have done, so don't even think about it." He encouraged His disciples to see big visions, dream big dreams, and accomplish big things. We should do the same for those who labor with us, and not discourage them by our own misgivings, inhibitions or lack of faith.

Sheepdogs Among the Flock

Let's believe God to put people together who complement each other when it comes to their strengths and weaknesses, and who celebrate and encourage one another in what they do well, and who help and support one another in areas where they don't.

A great professional basketball player and coach described this when he was talking about his college team during his senior year at school. None of the players had it all together, but each one of them could do certain things exceptionally well. They emphasized their strengths, they managed their weaknesses, and they went all the way to the NCAA championship game. We can do great things when we work together.

When new staff members come on board, faithful sheepdogs are supportive. Even though the person who is hired may not be a choice you would have made, you need to stand behind your pastor and work hard to make sure the newcomer has the best reception they could possibly have among the sheep. Your response will make a big difference here. Help new people help your pastor by making them welcome.

There are two extremes that are especially dangerous in the area of comparisons. On one extreme, if it appears that you are not as talented or gifted as a new person in a certain area, you may find yourself cast down in condemnation. On the other extreme, if you think you are better than the new person in one or more areas, you may be tempted to become lifted up in pride. Neither of these scenarios will help you do what God has called you to do, nor will they help the person who is supposed to be working with you to fulfill the Lord's purpose.

CLOSENESS, BUT NOT FAMILIARITY

Here's another trap the sheepdog must avoid: familiarity with the shepherd. I don't have to live with the shepherd, eat with him or visit his house to know him. Respect and high regard can be maintained in any relationship without becoming familiar and casual. I never refer to Pastor Parsley by his first name. He never refers to me by mine. I don't interrupt him, either in a private meeting or in a church service. In a formal situation, I don't have anything to say without obtaining leave to do so. I don't pray for him in a meeting without his approval. I rarely touch him unless he initiates it. We have a professional relationship that enables us to work together to achieve a goal that is bigger than either of us, bigger than both of us and bigger than all the church put together.

I realize that different customs prevail at different places, so if you have different guidelines at your church, that's all right with me. I'm just telling you what works where I work. Here's why it's so important: regardless of how long I have been at my post, I need to remember that when the pastor speaks, he's speaking to me, too. Certainly, there are advantages to being a senior staff member that others haven't yet achieved, but the rules apply to me as well as anyone else. I wear a name badge at work—everyone does. I get there on time and don't leave before I'm supposed to leave. I come to services early, as all the elders are expected to do, and stay after the service to pray with people at the altar unless I am needed elsewhere. This is the work that I am called and anointed to do.

WORK, NOT WORRY

Work is spiritual, and it is a gift from God. Adam received this gift in the garden before the fall. God told our first ancestor to dress and keep the garden, which meant to work it and guard it. We don't know exactly what kind of work this involved, but we know it did not involve laboring by the sweat of his brow to try to produce a living. Worry, anxiety and fear were unknown. Labor may have resulted in fatigue, but exhaustion was a foreign concept to Adam—inconceivable to him.

Our labor should be fulfilling to us, not filled with grief and anxiety. I have always maintained that work never killed anyone, but worrying about your work can be deadly. Everyone has physical, emotional and mental limits. While it is true that most of us may live and die without ever really finding out what our limits are, we realize that there are certain things we cannot and should not do.

What does a faithful sheepdog do when asked to do something he feels he cannot or should not do? Is it ever all right to refuse a task that needs to be accomplished? I don't think there are definitive rules in this area, and I think most of the time when a job needs to be done, you can find the grace to do it, and do it graciously.

If you find yourself in a position where you cannot do some assignment, explain why immediately and honestly. If you feel fatigue racing toward exhaustion, say so. If you find you need time off, schedule it.

When you do have time off from the demands of ministry, be sure to spend that time doing something that enables you to unwind—something that is fun, as well as redemptive. Everyone has different preferences in this area. For me, it includes something besides spending countless hours watching television or playing computer games.

Here is another principle that will help the humble sheepdog stay refreshed—keep your priorities straight. Don't allow your work to pull you away from the Lord, and don't make your work your lord. If your only satisfaction comes from your work and not your relationships, you have started down a slope it will be difficult to ascend.

A DISTANCE RACE

The Christian life is a marathon, not a sprint. God has moved heaven and earth to get you in the right place at the right time, so don't interrupt your service by disqualifying yourself or keeling over before you get to the finish line. God wants you to burn hot, but He also wants you to burn for many years. As an old farmer told me, he'd rather wear out than rust out or blow out.

Sheepdogs Among the Flock

Another baseball metaphor is appropriate here. When I was a kid, pitchers were not the specialists they have become in today's professional game. There were no such things as closers, short relievers and long relievers. There were only starters and relief pitchers. Many times, a relief pitcher was an unsuccessful starter who was recycled into that role. Starters were encouraged to pitch as long as they could in a game—there were no pitch counts and no coaches checking pitch speeds. If a pitcher was retiring batters, he stayed in the game, and if he wasn't, he came out.

The way pitchers dealt with this was by pacing themselves. They wouldn't throw fastballs all day long, but would vary their pitches and save their best stuff for when they had a deciding count on a batter. They weren't doing less than their best, but they were using their heads and not just their arms.

In the same way, we need to pace ourselves for the long run in God's service. I want to be a good servant, but I want to be good for a long time. I want to shine like a star, not just blaze like a flare, or even worse, blow up like a firecracker.

TAKE CARE OF YOURSELF

I'm certainly no medical doctor, and nothing I could say should be considered a substitute for advice from a medical professional, but I have observed some things over the years that spell trouble. Here are some signals that you may be reaching a breaking point physically or emotionally:

- Repeated or persistent physical symptoms
- Sleeplessness
- Irritability or outbursts of anger
- Moodiness or depression
- Anxiety or panic
- Forgetfulness
- Erratic or unprecedented changes in behavior

If you notice these things, or what is more likely, if your spouse or a coworker notices them, it's time for a break or at least a change of routine. A visit to your doctor wouldn't be a bad idea, either. Don't risk your physical or emotional health for one more project or one more meeting. It's healthy to be able to say, "That's enough."

Paul said in 1 Timothy 4:8: *"For bodily exercise profits a little, but godliness is profitable in all things...."*

A different rendering of this passage helps us understand that bodily exercise doesn't last very long, so we have to engage in it regularly to obtain any benefit from it. Don't try to deny it—you and I both know it's true from painful, personal experience—and it's more painful in your fifties than in your twenties.

Our bodies all play dirty tricks on us, and the older we get, the dirtier the tricks become. We can play some tricks of our own by refusing to conform to a slow-moving and sedentary lifestyle that has become commonplace just about everywhere.

This can be particularly troublesome for those in ministry, since ministers spend a lot of time sitting: in meetings, in church services, in offices, in vehicles and in homes. Our girths have become great and our behinds have become broad as a result. Get up, get out and get moving—it's not just a lifestyle choice, it's a matter of life and longevity.

When I was in elementary school, the government came up with the four food groups. Those guidelines were replaced with the food pyramid, and yet again with the so-called healthy plate. Even though recent evidence indicates that much of what the government has told us for decades about diet and nutrition has been wrong, I always liked the four food groups, and developed an affinity for them. In fact, after all these years, I can still recall what they are: fat, sugar, salt and white flour. And all of these staples find their greatest expression in culinary delights like doughnuts, cinnamon rolls and similar pastries. What could be better?

Another problem ministers encounter is that their schedules are often at odds with healthy eating habits. Hectic days and nights lend themselves to putting off eating until hunger is extreme, then overindulging in food that is immediately available and may taste good, but is not good for you. In addition, many ministers don't eat before services, eating late at night instead, when choices may be few and the temptation to overeat may be compelling.

I remember one particularly busy day when I had a number of hospital calls to make throughout the city. My route home after my last stop would take me past a favorite fast food place, known for its big specialty hamburgers. I had not eaten since morning, and when I got to the joint their famous burgers were on sale, two for something—I don't remember how much, and I didn't care. My plan was to eat one for dinner and then eat the other one later.

I came to my senses in a nearby parking lot, licking the leftover condiments off the wrapper of the second hamburger, which had mysteriously disappeared in the same way the first one had. I had even eaten all the sesame seeds that fell off the buns. Perhaps you have had a similar experience.

There are other gastronomic pitfalls for those in ministry. Sometimes people want to bless those who serve them in ministry by making cookies, baking pies or presenting you with other desserts. Those giving you these gifts will be sure to ask you if you enjoyed them, and you don't want to appear ungrateful for something sincerely given.

And then there are the unavoidable church dinners. Those who prepare the food for these events will be waiting breathlessly to see if you tried their specialty, and they will want to know whether or not you liked it. Of course, the only correct answer is a resounding *yes* to both.

I can sum all this up: start your exercise regimen by pushing back from the table or the buffet bar. Exercise something other than your fingers and jaws. Sit less and walk more. Have less anxiety and more activity. Live a long and healthy life so you can accomplish all God told you to do.

CHAPTER 20

Positioning and Training

It is a well-known fact that you shouldn't give a dog a tree-climbing job. They just weren't made to perform that task. All the investment of time and training in the world won't increase their proficiency at it. What is worse, they will become distraught because they can't do what they are being expected to do.

One of the principles that will lead to success in any organization is to put the right people in the right places, which will position them to succeed rather than fail. I am certain that pastors do not intend for people in their churches to fall short in any area. Why, then, are there so many frustrations and failures among those who help them?

KNOW WHAT YOU'RE GOOD AT DOING

I firmly believe that many sheepdogs are not being used to their potential in the body of Christ. One reason is that many of the helpers with the greatest potential have not even been identified, and they are still waiting for the right opportunity to fulfill the call upon their lives. In other cases, sheepdogs are already engaged in the work of the kingdom, but are either doing things improperly or engaged in tasks for which they are neither called nor equipped. Many sheepdogs will do whatever they are asked willingly, even if they aren't particularly skilled in that area. If they are left in that area indefinitely, they will become discouraged and the seeds for discontent will eventually be sown.

There is not much I haven't either been involved in or exposed to in church work. I have either overseen or served in nurseries, children's ministry, youth ministry, prayer ministry, evangelism, outreach, pastoral care, music, the business office, platform ministry, teaching and preaching, administration, Christian education, sound, television, hospitality, guest services, facilities, special meetings and just about everything else. (I have never flown a church aircraft, for which we can all thank God.) I have never asked to do anything that I have done, and I have always learned a lot in every ministry situation I have encountered.

What I like to do and what I am anointed to do is not always what I have an opportunity to do, but whatever I am asked to do, I will do to the best of my ability. My greatest strength, though—and the greatest likelihood of achieving satisfaction in my work—is in the areas where I have been especially anointed to serve.

When I was in Little League, I loved to go to the baseball field whenever I had the chance. I seldom had the privilege of going to a batting cage, so anytime I could convince someone to throw me some pitches for batting practice, it was extra special. One day we were at the field, and I was swinging at about twenty pitches at a time without a break. An older gentleman was watching me, along with my father. I batted right-handed, and just about every pitch I hit would go to the gap between left and center field.

"That's where his strength is," I heard the older man say. "He's getting out in front of those balls and hitting them in front of the plate. That's where his strength is."

I didn't realize what he was talking about at the time, since I was caught up in the rare chance to be able to swing freely. Now I realize that even though I could have hit those pitches all over the field, there was a sweet spot that enabled me to connect more regularly than anywhere else.

The same thing is true in ministry. There are things any sheepdog can do, but there are certain areas where they are created to excel. A wise shepherd will help his helpers find those areas where they thrive, and he will arrange circumstances so they can serve in the places where they are particularly effective.

There are times when this is not always possible. Sometimes vacancies or emergencies cause people to be pressed into service for which they may not feel particularly capable or comfortable. Whether or not they succeed in these areas depends on the support they get from the shepherd, along with the knowledge that such an assignment will not last forever. If this happens to you, do the best you can for as long as you can, and stay in touch with your shepherd so you know how the situation is developing.

Sheepdogs Among the Flock

There was a time when I was asked to lead praise and worship at our church. Some people probably thought that was odd, since I neither read music nor played an instrument. However, I was not bashful. (Enthusiasm can make up for a lot of deficiencies.) I was diligent about letting those who were following me on the platform know where I wanted to go, and I was animated enough to keep people engaged. They may have only been watching to see what I would do next, but it seemed like they were paying attention.

Other people were able to rehearse with the band and select appropriate music, but I was the person who was actually out in front. I could do it, and I did do it, but it's not what I'm called to do. When we finally hired a full-time praise and worship leader, people came up to me and expressed their disappointment that I was not still leading. I told them not to feel sorry for me, because I was the happiest person on the planet.

HONORING MEN AND WOMEN OF GOD

As a helper, there is no substitute for spending time with your leaders to discover how to be a responsible and faithful servant of God. When I first came to World Harvest Church, Pastor Parsley told me, "If you want to be a church man, you have to be around church men." He was right.

Many important concepts can be successfully transmitted to people in formal classroom settings, but values, either for personal life or ministry, are more *caught* than *taught*.

Most often, this *catching* comes in informal situations that cannot be reproduced in a classroom, and sometimes not even in a church service. That is why it is important for pastors to allow others to be with them so they can learn from them in a variety of settings.

This is one of the very best ways for helpers to learn how to behave, both in and out of the house of God. I don't mean that a pastor needs to always have an entourage of people following him around like a bunch of baby ducks, but young men and women need a chance to see how ministry works behind the platform, as well as on it.

We ought to give honor to men and women of God. I don't believe we can do too much for them. Opening doors, carrying briefcases, doing errands and other such activities are no problem for those who have a heart to serve. I have had the opportunity to do it myself, and never felt that it was a burden or somehow beneath me. But I have seen this carried to an extreme that is unnecessary, and, in my opinion, displeases God.

I'm happy to know there are those who will open doors, carry Bibles, and arrange details that a minister should not have to worry about, especially when they are getting ready to preach. These are courtesies that help them stay focused and not be distracted by extraneous things. Sometimes security personnel are needed because there are so many bizarre things that people try to do to those they perceive as famous. (If things keep going this direction, I don't doubt we will soon see some zealous but misguided individuals starting fan clubs and collecting trading cards of preachers.)

But when I see a person enter the auditorium like a rock star, I can't help but wonder if all that attention is really necessary. I'm tempted to think someone is just trying to make an impression with an abundance of sound and fury instead of depending on the anointing upon their life.

A long time ago, a guest at our church was trying to impress us with this kind of behavior. My pastor took him aside after the service and said, "Brother, we don't have celebrities here. We have men of God."

TEACHING AND TRAINING ARE PART OF THE JOB

Most people who are genuinely called to public ministry have an ability to teach or preach. That is part of the equipment that goes with their calling. If passable preaching were all that is necessary for someone to be successful in ministry, we would have a lot less failures in the body of Christ.

I have observed that where most ministers experience problems is not in their speaking ability on the platform, but in how they relate to people off the platform. You don't have to be a great preacher to be a good pastor, but you do have to be able to relate to people in a way that communicates love and concern for them in their everyday lives. If you come across as stiff, cold, uncaring, inattentive and formal in interpersonal interactions, you will have a tough time being successful in pastoral ministry.

I love to hear good preaching, and I admire those who are gifted in that area. I will listen to a masterful message and ask myself, "Whence cometh this revelation?" Anointed preaching is more necessary in the church than ever before. However, many sheepdogs will live and die without getting close to a pulpit. This does not mean they are of no value to the body.

Paul said in 1 Corinthians 12:23-24 that the parts of the body that are uncomely may be more important than the ones that are seen. For every person involved in pulpit ministry, there may be a score or more who are involved behind the scenes, making sure the pulpit ministry can be heard and is effective.

But how are the helpers going to know how to behave and how to serve if they don't ever have the chance to learn? Baby boomers, now in power in just about every sphere of our culture, are perhaps the worst generation when it comes to raising up those who will follow them, because of their desire to attain power and to hold on to it. We should not relinquish the reins until the appropriate time, but eventually that time will come, and the light will need to be kept burning by someone else. The job they do will be directly related to how well we trained them.

One minister always brings one or two young men with him whenever he visits our church. He lets them accompany him not just so they can carry his Bible, but so they have the opportunity to see how an experienced minister acts and reacts in a variety of situations. This proximity also gives him the chance to observe the young men and provide instruction and correction when it's necessary. My pastor and others do the same thing.

If this kind of guidance is not forthcoming, it can cause young preachers and other helpers to think that they can do whatever seems right in their eyes. This will lead to all kinds of disappointments in the body of Christ. Regardless of how talented or capable they may seem, even the best helpers need to be trained.

Training is not the same as teaching, as many parents have discovered to their dismay. Teaching means to instruct or to impart information. Training, on the other hand, means to instruct by exercise or to drill. It involves not only giving direction, but making the trainee do what you have instructed them to do, and then inspecting the results. This has to be done over and over again in order for the training to become a part of the trainee's behavior.

Every spring, major league baseball players report to spring training. They don't call it spring teaching—and for good reason. All the players go through the same drills, whether they are veterans or rookies. They do the same things again and again until they don't even have to think about how they are going to react during a game situation. Training causes their responses to become intuitive rather than reasoned. You don't have time to think when a batted ball is whistling toward your head at a hundred miles an hour. The players don't resent their training, because they know their skills must be sharpened to help them experience success on the field.

As ministry helpers, we should never stop learning, and never be irritated by the guidance and correction we receive. We should also welcome opportunities to be accountable for our actions and decisions. It is all a part of our training, so that we can be successful in fulfilling our calling.

When tending natural sheep, shepherds are in constant communication with their dogs. The same should be true with God's sheep. Without some form of regular contact, the most loyal and skilled sheepdogs may lose focus.

WHEN THE SHEEPDOG NEEDS HELP

Pastors are extremely busy with the demands of ministry. When an area is working as it should, it is a great relief for a pastor, since he doesn't feel the need to babysit that area as he would if it were in trouble. However, this can lead to neglect on the part of the pastor, as difficulties may develop without his knowledge.

The sheep appear to be at peace. The sheepdog gives no indication help is needed. Everything is good, right? Not always. There are two things the shepherd can do to look well to the ways of the flock.

First, the shepherd who is diligent in prayer will develop sensitivity in the spirit realm that will tell him when someone or something is in trouble, even though there is no natural indication of it.

Sheepdogs Among the Flock

Next, the shepherd can arrange to interact with his sheepdogs on a regular basis. This could be as formal as a regular meeting, or as informal as the shepherd and his helper crossing each other's paths before or after a service, at a church function, or on some other occasion. In this way, questions can be asked and answered to help the shepherd know how things really are, instead of how they just appear to be.

If a sheepdog is in trouble, why wouldn't he just let the shepherd know? There may be lots of reasons. Pride may be an issue—the sheepdog doesn't want to admit there are things he can't handle by himself. There may be situations the sheepdog is so close to he can't see. In these cases, a person with a perspective from outside the situation can help. The sheepdog may feel any call for help will cause him to be seen as a failure or not up to the task in some way.

If a sheepdog doesn't have enough confidence to ask the shepherd for help, there needs to be a serious reevaluation of their relationship. In addition, if the only kind of feedback a sheepdog ever gets from the shepherd is negative, he will become gun-shy, and a gun-shy dog has little value in the field.

Some friends of ours had a young beagle they asked us to help train. Beagles are bred to hunt rabbits. Some may be house pets, but their purpose as a breed is primarily to hunt. We took the dog with us to hunt with our veteran rabbit hounds. The young dog showed interest and intelligence, and we thought she had the potential to be a fine hunting dog.

We needed to see how the dog responded to gunfire. While it was nearby, my father took out his .22 pistol and fired it as a test. We never saw the dog again until we got back to our friend's house and found it curled up in its box. Something happened, probably very early in the dog's life, that caused it to be traumatized by loud noises. Some dogs can overcome this, but this one never did. Consequently, it never fulfilled its potential as a rabbit hound.

Can people be traumatized this way? Yes, they can—and I'm convinced that is the reason some of them never fulfill their purpose. If all work and no play makes Jack a dull boy, all criticism and no praise makes Shep an unproductive sheepdog.

Are there ever occasions where a shepherd is consistently callous and critical toward those who help him? I have been blessed to serve a pastor who has a passion for excellence, but who also has a forgiving heart and a generous spirit. In contrast, I have heard of some situations in churches which, if true, would be a nightmare for anyone who is called to help. Under those conditions, gun-shy sheepdogs would be the rule rather than the exception.

How can gun-shy sheepdogs come to the point that they are confident enough to ask for help? Keep in mind that shepherds don't always give the impression of approachability. They have lots of responsibilities and their time needs to be respected. However, a genuine shepherd always responds positively to a genuine need that is appropriately expressed.

The best suggestion I can make is don't wait. Get the help you need sooner rather than later. This may require multiple requests at different times. If answers are not forthcoming from one person, ask someone else. Somebody has the information that you need. Unfortunately, in a busy ministry with many competing priorities, it may become your task to discover who that is and how to get it. Be relentless in the pursuit of your goal.

Several of my wife's family members served in the United States Navy. Without exception, they affirmed that there were three possible ways to accomplish a task: my way, your way, and the Navy way. Sometimes the Navy way seemed to be the least likely to succeed, but when you are in the Navy, the Navy way is the right way.

It's the same for sheepdogs. When working in someone else's vineyard, be sure to find out how he wants the vines tended. Chances are he will want things done differently than you would do them. When things are not done appropriately, which will inevitably happen, correction will be necessary. This is a fundamental principle of growth and grace and life. It is unavoidable and inescapable. You don't have to like it, but you will have to endure it—and you should learn to profit from it.

One of the most redemptive things a shepherd can do when bringing correction to those who work with him is to affirm his confidence in them either before, during or after the correction. Most sheepdogs are eager to please, and the knowledge that they have displeased the shepherd will be a burden to them. If the shepherd becomes angry or unkind or simply withdraws, the sheepdog's confidence will spiral downward along with his effectiveness.

Parents who correct their children must never do so in anger and should always affirm their love for and approval of their child even though they do not approve of a particular action, decision or attitude. This takes a lot more work than simply yelling at a child when he or she does something wrong. Conscientious shepherds will keep this in mind when administering correction to even the most reluctant or recalcitrant sheepdogs.

Sometimes it hurts to be helped. I'll mind the hurt a lot less if I know I still have the confidence of my shepherd after I have recovered.

Everybody needs to know that somebody believes in them. Part of a shepherd's responsibility is to be an encourager, not only to the sheep but also to the sheepdogs. A sincere expression of confidence from the shepherd will go a long way toward motivating a sincere sheepdog for a long time. Most sheepdogs don't require a lot of attention, but a pat on the head or a scratch behind the ears from their shepherd can make all the difference in the world to them.

I've mentioned this elsewhere, but it bears repeating: a clear understanding beforehand will avoid a misunderstanding afterward. Another way of saying much the same thing is that assumptions are the lowest form of human knowledge. Assumptions also require little effort — maybe that's why we make them so often. When in doubt, ask. If you have forgotten something or the instructions are still unclear, ask again.

If you don't have the information you need, you are not stupid, you are only ignorant. If the information you need is available and you don't ask, you are both ignorant and stupid.

If you can't describe what is expected of you in a sentence or two, you probably don't know, and you are probably not accomplishing much. But even if you know what you're supposed to be doing right now, in the real world expectations can and do change. Make sure you stay abreast of what is expected of you, and how you are doing at what you are supposed to be doing.

A thirteen-year-old boy had a great job mowing the lawn for a doctor in his town. One Saturday afternoon he called the doctor's house.

"I'd like to know if you need somebody to mow your yard."

"No, we already have someone who mows our yard," the doctor said.

"Is he doing a good job?" the boy asked.

"Well, yes, we're happy with the job he does," the doctor said.

"Okay, thank you very much," the boy said before he hung up the phone.

He found out what he wanted to know. You can be more subtle than that, but it never hurts to check up on yourself.

MINISTRY TASKS CAN BE MOVING TARGETS

Change is inevitable, and it is often a good thing. Someone once said a rut is simply a grave with both ends knocked out of it. Managing change is not just a ministry skill, but a life skill. Things are going to change whether you want them to or not, and regardless of how desperately you try to make them stay the way they are. Cosmetic surgeons the world over have become wealthy because of this.

When expectations of what you are supposed to be doing change, you need to know about it. One of the most damaging things that can happen in a relationship between shepherds and sheepdogs is when a faithful subordinate receives an assignment and labors faithfully to complete it, only to find out after it's done that it is no longer needed. The longer a project takes and the more difficult it is, the more necessary it becomes for the sheepdog to be apprised of any changes in the project's status. It can be extremely frustrating and disappointing for a sheepdog to discover that their labor has essentially been in vain.

Hitting a stationary target requires a certain amount of expertise, but hitting a moving target with regularity requires even more skill and more practice. Hitting a target moving through three dimensions is even tougher. That's why hunters have more difficulty shooting birds than rabbits. Rabbits run along the ground and have a stationary visual background upon which they are moving. Birds, on the other hand, move through the air, and the background of sky makes their speed, trajectory and distance more difficult to judge, making wing-shooting wild birds one of the most challenging of all the shooting sports.

The more variables there are in your assignment, the more likely it is you will experience difficulty in achieving a satisfactory outcome. Do your best to nail down expectations before the project begins. This isn't always possible, because the shepherd may not know exactly what he wants until the work is underway. In most cases, even if he doesn't know what it is, he will be certain of what it isn't! Offer him some choices, and as he makes those choices, your expectations will become clearer.

Don't just throw up your hands in frustration and say that you can't do anything. What you are experiencing is just a more sophisticated version of the children's game Hot or Cold. Do you remember? In this game, you select an object, a number, or something that can be reasonably guessed, but you don't tell your companion what you have chosen. They have to discover it by you telling them if their guesses are hot or cold. You can't tell them what it is, but you can tell them if they're moving in the right direction.

This may seem like a strange way to do kingdom business, but not everything involving God's vision for a local church or worldwide ministry is always cut and dried. Sometimes there is a lot of trial and error that has to go on before the right solution is found—especially if it's a project or initiative for which there is no example or precedent.

Difficult tasks take time. Impossible tasks take a little longer. But as a properly positioned and carefully trained sheepdog, you will find that those things that seemed impossible aren't really out of the question—they just take a little more time and effort. God's people are worth it.

CHAPTER 21

Other Anointed Helpers

There are many anointed helpers in the Bible who were obviously appointed to assist God's leaders—sometimes for a specific task or occasion, and sometimes for decades. I want to point out some pertinent details about a select few. You will recognize some of their names, while others are almost completely overlooked.

THE UNNAMED MATCHMAKER

One of the greatest examples of a faithful helper can be found in Genesis 24, where Abraham commissions one of his servants to go to Mesopotamia to find a wife for his son Isaac. His story involves customs and cultures that are unknown to most of us in the western world, but it is an important example of how to properly fulfill a position of trust.

This man was an unnamed servant, even though some think he might be Eliezer of Damascus, who is identified by Abraham earlier. He is described here only as Abraham's eldest servant. It should be noted that the term eldest may refer to rank rather than age—eldest in this sense meaning first or head servant. In any case, he was in a position of great influence, having proven his reliability in Abraham's household for many years, and was a capable administrator of the patriarch's possessions.

His assignment was to go to Abraham's relatives and bring back a suitable wife for Isaac, the promised descendant and heir of all that Abraham had. This was no minor undertaking. The man took ten camels burdened with wealth and started on his journey immediately, even though he had only the most rudimentary of instructions. Abraham obviously had confidence in his judgment in important matters, since his choice of a bride would impact everything that happened to Abraham's progeny for generations.

The servant trusted God to give him good success, and his prayer was answered in a way that exceeded even his expectations. His efforts resulted in Rebekah returning with him to a land she had never seen to become the bride of a man she had never met. Her only knowledge of Isaac was the word of a faithful servant. His trustworthiness was essential on both ends of the equation. Abraham trusted him, as did Rebekah—and God's plan for His people was advanced by a servant without a name, but with a great reputation both on earth and in heaven.

JOSEPH

Joseph is not usually thought of as a helper, but everywhere he went, he was a first-class servant. His father Jacob regarded him as a favorite, but also trusted young Joseph to give him accurate reports about what his brothers were doing. That was undoubtedly part of the reason his brothers hated him—because as long as Joseph was around, their activities were sure to be reported back to their father.

When Joseph was purchased by Potiphar, it wasn't long before he noticed his servant's industrious and conscientious character, which led to Joseph's advancement. In contrast to so many people today who trumpet their status as victims, we see no indication that Joseph bemoaned his fate while serving in Potiphar's household. Before long, he was running the place, and as it turned out, he was more trustworthy than the military man's own wife.

After he was falsely accused and relegated to prison, Joseph became the most trusted and reliable prisoner in the entire institution. He kept being knocked down to the bottom, but as the old saying goes, cream always rises to the top. The time came when he was elevated to second in command in all of Egypt. Everywhere he went, Joseph served with distinction.

Joseph's life is an example of how advancement is available to anyone who will apply themselves to the tasks they find at hand. You wouldn't know it from listening to some in our popular culture, but honesty, hard work and good behavior still yield positive results.

Sheepdogs Among the Flock

DAVID

David is most commonly known as the great warrior king of Israel, but we must not ignore his beginnings as a shepherd who was responsible for keeping his father's sheep. David wasn't exactly voted most likely to succeed among those in his family. In fact, when Samuel came to Jesse's house to anoint the next king of Israel, it seems that David was even overlooked by his own father until Samuel asked if Jesse had any other sons.

David looked after his father's flock as though it were his. He defended the sheep from both a lion and a bear, as well as other threats that he did not mention. Shepherds were not generally the most highly regarded group in society, but in a time when wealth was measured by the size of a man's flocks and herds, they were more important than their contemporaries would admit. A good shepherd would increase the value of a flock. An indifferent or bad shepherd could bring a householder to ruin by his neglect of the sheep.

Even more importantly, when David became one of Saul's servants, he went about fulfilling his duties with distinction. This continued even while Saul was trying to kill him. Despite the most despicable of plots to bring him down, David never sought to retaliate against the man who became his relentless enemy. On two occasions, David had the opportunity to kill Saul, but he refused to stretch his hand out against the one upon whom the anointing of God had once rested.

This is a stunning rebuke to all those helpers who would rise up against those who have given them an opportunity for any kind of service in the house of God. We must resist the temptation to speak or act in a way contrary to God's purposes by criticizing or harming those who have been over us in the Lord—even when they do things wrong.

Sometimes leaders stray from the path they formerly followed. Sometimes they fall from the grace they have been given—and sometimes they do it in spectacular fashion. We must always remember that first and foremost they are God's servants, and it is before God that they will ultimately stand or fall. God forbid that we should do anything to interfere with God Himself dealing with them according to righteousness and ultimate truth.

JONATHAN

Jonathan had a helper, an unnamed armorbearer, but Jonathan himself, the son of King Saul, was also a helper. In his case, he was a covenant partner of David.

This may have seemed an unlikely partnership, but there was something about the character of David and Jonathan that enabled them to walk together in agreement. We must realize that in some cases it is not the work of men, but the hand of God that is involved in putting people together. Some meetings are not coincidences, but divine appointments arranged by God to further His purposes.

Sheepdogs Among the Flock

Jonathan was a major source of encouragement to David during some of the greatest trials of David's life. He interceded with his father Saul on David's behalf. He told him of the intentions of his father when Saul was determined to kill David. He came to David in exile and gave him a message of hope, even though he knew it would displease the king.

Jonathan didn't see David as a threat or a competitor, but as a true friend and loyal confidant. His confidence in David was rewarded, since David confirmed his covenant promise to look after his friend's family even after Jonathan was dead. Such commitment is little known today, but honorable men in every age fulfill their words with corresponding deeds, not just good intentions or empty promises.

DANIEL

Daniel was a young man among the captives of Judah brought to the court of Babylon to be trained as administrators in the court of Nebuchadnezzar. He maintained a testimony of faith in God and a reputation as a man of integrity throughout his long life, which spanned the entire time from his captivity until after the overthrow of the Babylonian empire.

Daniel provides us a prime example of righteous service in an unrighteous regime. He faithfully fulfilled his duties, but never once compromised his faith in God. There were times when his life was threatened because of his convictions, but he remained steadfast, and maintained a standard of attitude and behavior that all of us would do well to emulate. He was an invaluable advisor to every king who consulted him, and he provided counsel that was as wise as it was timely. He was not afraid to speak the truth regardless of the cost. He was recognized and rewarded by even the most ungodly of rulers.

Daniel exemplified lofty ideals of unselfish and honorable service in the area of the public square. His example is more important than ever before. Public service used to be an opportunity to guide policy and influence culture in a way that did the most good and the least harm. Now it is seen by many as an avenue by which to accumulate wealth and power for selfish purposes.

BARUCH

Another helper is mentioned in Jeremiah 36, named Baruch. He was Jeremiah's scribe, or secretary. It appears that on certain occasions, Baruch was the one who wrote what God gave Jeremiah to say, and at least once Baruch had the job of going to the house of the Lord to read the prophetic word of judgment God gave Jeremiah. This national rebuke was reported to the king, who ordered both Jeremiah and Baruch to be arrested, but God hid them.

There is perhaps no position regarded as more entry level, at least in office environments, than a humble secretary. This is despite the fact that in some places, they know more about how the whole outfit is run than anyone else, sometimes including the owner or CEO.

In Baruch's case, he was called to stand in for the prophet and undergo a portion of his persecutions. This is an important lesson for all helpers. If you share in the leader's publicity, you can also expect to share in his notoriety. Don't let either of these things move you or keep you from doing what God has called you to do. And regardless of what you do, even if it seems as insignificant as typing letters, when you are handling the word of God, it has life-changing implications.

OBADIAH

1 Kings 18 gives us another snapshot of a righteous man laboring in a wicked vineyard. Obadiah was the head of Ahab's household, and was serving during the drought prophesied by Elijah. Ahab chose Obadiah to assist him in attempting to find any water sources that were still available. It was during this mission that Obadiah encountered Elijah, who told him to tell Ahab that he wanted to meet him.

Obadiah was a man who feared God, but he knew something of Elijah's reputation for being here and then gone in an instant. He was afraid that as soon as he told Ahab where Elijah was, the Spirit of God would snatch him away, causing Obadiah to be in jeopardy before the mercurial and impatient Ahab. After receiving assurances from Elijah, Obadiah did as he was told, and Ahab and Elijah met face to face.

As a helper, you may be asked to do something you would rather not do. But when you know you are acting on God's orders, and not out of your own intellect or understanding, you can be sure you will be protected and blessed as a result of your obedience.

Obadiah fulfilled a critical function in enabling Elijah to see Ahab personally and deliver a challenge to him that would demonstrate conclusively to all Israel that God Almighty was the God who heard and answered prayer. Any other deities were not gods at all, even the ones who had royal approval.

HUSHAI

Hushai the Archite is first seen during David's escape from Jerusalem during Absalom's rebellion in 2 Samuel 15:32-37. He came to David with his garments rent and earth upon his head, intending to follow his king wherever he went. However, David had another plan. He directed Hushai to go into Jerusalem and announce his allegiance to Absalom, for the purpose of defeating the counsel of Ahithophel, as well as being David's eyes and ears in the court. This he did to perfection. In this passage, he was called David's friend—and even Absalom acknowledged him as such. In 1 Chronicles 27:33, Hushai is again identified as the king's friend.

ZABUD

The term *friend* is used rather loosely in the present age. In times past, a friend was not just someone with whom you had an acquaintance or who acknowledged your presence on social media, but a person who stood by you in seasons of difficulty, as well as during good times. A friend saw you at your worst, as well as at your best, and loved you just the same. A friend was a person whose counsel you could trust and with whom you could share confidences without hesitation and without shame.

This was so important to Solomon that when the list of his advisors and officers was recorded in 1 Kings 4:5, a man named Zabud, the son of Nathan, was not only designated as the principal officer, but also as the king's friend.

Why was it so important to mention whom the king regarded as his friend? It's important because it's lonely at the top. The big chair behind the big desk may be in a big office that's always bustling and full of people, but it can also be the loneliest place in the building. An employer, chairman, president or pastor can have lots of associates, subordinates or workers, but not very many people who can truly be called friends.

Most people who call themselves your friends are actually only acquaintances. True friends are few and develop far less frequently. This may not seem like such an issue when your circle of acquaintances is large, but as the number of people who truly qualify as friends diminishes, the importance of each one grows.

BEING A HELPER AND A FRIEND

A select few who are helpers may be chosen by God to become friends of those whose responsibilities far surpass anything you may ever know. Here are a few ways you can be helpful to them as a friend.

Respect their time and space. Friends are available when they are needed, but don't hang around when they're not. Keep your distance, and be aware of the privacy needs of those in authority. Access is the most important thing they can give you. Respect it, and you will get more of it. Abuse it, and the door will close to you, and possibly upon you.

Keep confidences. Those in positions of power and authority have the same needs as others. One of the biggest needs people have is to belong. Sometimes a leader just needs a listening ear to help them feel normal or to confirm that the doubts and fears they are facing are not out of the ordinary. But nobody will confide in you if you don't keep their revelations to yourself. Your proximity to someone in authority assumes your confidentiality. You should never talk openly about what you hear privately. Proverbs 17:17 says, *A friend loves at all times…* Love covers—it does not expose.

Practice the art of being. Friends walk through seasons of life with others. You are not expected to supply an explanation for what defies explaining, or come up with a solution to every problem. Your presence can make a difference if you will just listen instead of talk. Job's friends were of more help to him when they were silent than when they spoke.

In times of stress or hardship, uncharacteristic behavior or unkind words should not surprise you. One of the times a true friend is needed most is when things are at their worst. Your estimation of the one who calls you a friend should not diminish just because you see them when they are less than their best. They may be without the makeup or the hairpiece, or with a house that's full of clutter or has laundry piled on the floor. That's one of the reasons they chose you to be with them—so you could see them the way they really are and not be shocked.

None of this is to say that we should ever condone ungodliness or unrighteous behavior. Friends don't make excuses to cover up sin. True friends are able to see what others cannot see and continue to love, to care and to pray. Blessed indeed is the shepherd who has someone like this near him.

NEW TESTAMENT DEACONS

One of the finest groups of helpers in the Bible is found in Acts 6, where the apostles arranged for a group of men to assist in the ministry of compassion that they oversaw in Jerusalem. Seven were in this original group, and they were appointed to act under the authority of the apostles to serve at tables where daily distribution of food was conducted. Even though they are not specifically called by that name

here, this is generally regarded as the first example of deacons in the church (the word *deacon* means servant or minister).

The qualifications for deacons are given in Acts 6:3, and
by Paul in 1 Timothy 3:8-13. Everyone who serves in any
capacity in the church would do well to review these characteristics from time to time to make sure they are measur-
ing up to the standard God requires for servants.

Since Paul is one of the most prominent figures in the
epistles, it should not be surprising that most of the examples of New Testament helpers are associated with him.

BARNABAS

Barnabas was a true helper in several different ways.
His name means *son of consolation*, and he was a great encourager. He sought Paul when he was in Tarsus and
brought him to Antioch to help lead that growing church.
Before that, Barnabas introduced Paul after his salvation experience to the leaders of the church in Jerusalem. He accompanied Paul on the first missionary journey. He also
gave sacrificially to continue the work of God. He may have
been identified later as a prophet, teacher and apostle, but
his work began as a helper.

PRISCILLA AND AQUILA

Priscilla and Aquila were also identified as helpers
along with Paul in the work of the Lord. They had a tent-
making enterprise in Corinth and welcomed Paul as he

worked alongside them in their craft while he was evangelizing in the city. Later, they would be instrumental in mentoring Apollos, who was a powerful preacher of the gospel. They hosted a church in their home, and Paul always had words of kind remembrance for them in his letters, calling them his helpers in Christ Jesus.

TIMOTHY

Perhaps Paul's best-known helper was Timothy, a man who was nurtured and discipled by Paul himself. Timothy received two of Paul's letters about church administration, which, along with Titus, are known as the pastoral epistles. Timothy traveled with Paul, ministered under his tutelage and eventually pastored in cities where Paul began churches. It must have been quite a relationship—one that should be copied everywhere by more experienced ministers and younger ones alike. Paul found a young man who was eager to receive what he was willing to give.

JOHN MARK

John Mark was a young man who had the honor of being a traveling companion of Paul and Barnabas on the first journey they undertook from Antioch. He was a nephew of Barnabas, and Acts 13:5 identifies him as their assistant, or servant. The group had not gone far when John Mark, known as John in this episode, left them and went back home to Jerusalem. We don't know why he departed from them, but it no doubt caused a great deal of difficulty for those he left behind.

When the time came for Paul and Barnabas to return to the churches they began during their first trip, Barnabas wanted to take John Mark with them again, but Paul wouldn't hear of it. They couldn't agree, so they split up. Paul and Silas went together, and Barnabas and John Mark went a different direction. The Bible says that Paul didn't want John Mark to go with him specifically because of his desertion on the earlier trip.

That could have been the end of the story, but God had other plans. Among Paul's final instructions to Timothy, we find these words in 2 Timothy 4:11:

Get Mark, and bring him with you, for he is profitable to me for the ministry.

This small sentence has powerful implications for all helpers everywhere. Put yourself in John Mark's place for a moment. He had the chance to serve two men who were pointed out by God Himself for a special assignment. He could have served with distinction through a history-making tour of the known world. Instead, he succumbed to the temptation to go back home. No doubt he felt as though he were a failure after that. I can only imagine the thoughts of doubt and defeat that assailed him.

While it is true that Barnabas continued to be his advocate, the family connection between them mitigated any future successes John Mark may have had. Paul didn't want him, and that must have preyed upon his thoughts and aspirations.

John Mark eventually became a trusted understudy of Peter and amassed a wealth of knowledge and experience that would later influence the gospel that would bear his name. But none of these accomplishments could completely erase the failure that he experienced as a very young man in a role for which he may not have been adequately prepared.

Paul was not a man to hold on to a grudge. We see a definite warming in his attitude toward John Mark in Colossians 4:10. But the final acceptance of one who was formerly rejected came when Paul asked Timothy to bring John Mark with him.

A FINAL WORD

Sheepdogs, helpers, deacons, ministers, servants—hear this: Your failure is not final. Your shortcomings don't define who you are. You may have done something that knocked you out of your lane and disqualified you from recognition for one event, but your life is not over. If you will be quick to repent and refuse to blame, if you will learn and grow and continue to position yourself for usefulness, God will open doors that no man can close. The time will come when those who rejected you, regardless of how justified they may have been, will recognize in you the same things that God does. They will say about you the same thing your Heavenly Father says: "You are profitable to Me for the ministry."

ENDNOTES

[1] Sumrall, Lester. "Minister's Meeting." Question and answer session, Canton, Ohio, 1984.

[2] Sumrall, Lester. *God's Blueprint for a Happy Home*. Green Forest, AR. New Leaf Press, 1995. p. 104.

[3] "Sheep Depredation." *Harrison News-Herald* (Cadiz, Ohio), 1971.

[4] Brown, Joe David. "A BIG MAN EVEN IN BIG D." SI.com. Accessed November 09, 2018. https://www.sci.com/vault/1963/01/21/604768/a-big-man-even-in-big-d.

[5] "A Quote from Romeo and Juliet." Goodreads. Accessed November 09, 2018. https://www.goodreads.com/quotes/405331-what-s-in-a-name-that-which-we-call-a-rose.

[6] "Man with No Name." Wikipedia. November 06, 2018. Accessed November 09, 2018. https://en.wikipedia.org/wiki/Man_with_No_Name.

[7] "If You Lie Down with Dogs, You Will Get Up with Fleas." The Free Dictionary. Accessed November 09, 2018. https://idioms.thefreedictionary.com/If you lie down with dogs, you will get up with fleas.

[8] Sumrall, Lester. "Minister's Meeting." Question and answer session, Canton, Ohio, 1984.

[9] Sumrall, Lester. *Pioneers of Faith*. Tulsa: Harrison House, 1995. p. 163.

[10] Ibid. p. 164.

[11] Wolff, Alexander. "The Shot: Duke and Christian Laettner Beat Kentucky." SI.com. Accessed November 09, 2018. https://www.si.com/vault/1992/12/28/127836/march-28-the-shot-heard-round-the-world-a-miraculous-last-second-play-lifted-duke-over-kentucky-in-perhaps-the-greatest-college-game-ever-played.

[12] "The Starfish Story: One Step towards Changing the World." EventsForChange. June 06, 2011. Accessed November 09, 2018. https://eventsforchange.wordpress.com/2011/06/05/the-starfish-story-one-step-towards-changing-the-world/.

[13] Mikkelson, David. "'Life Is Hard; It's Even Harder When You're Stupid'." Snopes.com. Accessed November 09, 2018. https://www.snopes.com/fact-check/words-of-wisdom.

[14] Saum, Von R. "Children's Ministry Seminar." Centerville, Ohio. 1982.

NEED HELP WRITING YOUR BOOK?

If you are writing a book, or you are interested in writing a book, we can help you! We can help you develop your book, write your book and edit your book. Any book worth writing is worth writing well! For more information, visit us at canfieldcommunication.com or billandpaulacanfield.com.

OTHER BOOKS

Other books by William C. Canfield: *Joined Together: A Celebration of Marriage*—a 32-page wedding ceremony that includes the necessary forms to keep all the information about an upcoming wedding in one place for easy reference. It is also intended to be a keepsake gift for the bride and groom at the conclusion of the wedding festivities.

To contact the author, visit canfieldcommunication.com or billandpaulacanfield.com.